"Praise" for *How to Win a Fight with a Conservative*

Listen to what the critics *aren't* saying:

"How dare this book try to make conservatives look like idiots. That's my job."

—*Michele Bachmann*

"I have people who have been studying this book, and they cannot believe what they're finding. It's huge! I believe the author has pulled one of the great cons in the history of politics."

—*Donald Trump*

"This book will lead directly to man-on-dog sex."

—*Rick Santorum*

"This book is what Paul Revere was trying to warn the British about when liberals tried to bring conservatives before death panels during the Revolutionary squirmish. Please refudiate."

—*Sarah Palin*

"There are three reasons why you should not buy this book. One, it's not funny. Two, it makes fun of

Republicans, and the third is … what's the third one there? I can't. The third one, I can't. Sorry. Oops."

—*Rick Perry*

"I've got this book in my prison cell, and it's f**king golden. I'm just not giving it up for f**king nothing."

—*Rod Blagojevich*

"We've tried everything from *Harry Potter* to *Heather Has Two Mommies*, but we've found that no book burns better than *How to Win a Fight with a Conservative*."

—*Pat Robertson*

"Anyone who reads this book is Hitler."

—*Glenn Beck*

HOW TO
WIN A
FIGHT WITH A
CONSERVATIVE

BY DANIEL KURTZMAN
www.FightConservatives.com

Published by Sourcebooks, Inc.
P.O. Box 4410, Naperville, Illinois 60567-4410
(630) 961-3900
Fax: (630) 961-2168
www.sourcebooks.com

Library of Congress Cataloging-in-Publication Data

Kurtzman, Daniel.
  How to win a fight with a conservative / by Daniel Kurtzman.
     p. cm.
  (alk. paper)
  1. Conservatism—United States. 2. Conservatism—United States—
Humor. I. Title.
  JC573.2.U6K873 2012
  320.520973—dc23

                    2012007573

          Printed and bound in Canada.
              WC 10 9 8 7 6 5 4 3

Dedication

FOR MY WIFE, LAURA;
MY SON, JOEL;
MY PARENTS, KEN AND CARYL;
AND MY BROTHER, TODD

Contents

Introduction   **xi**

Chapter 1: What It Means
to Be a Liberal   **1**
  What Breed of Liberal Are You?   4
  The Liberal Manifesto   12
  Rate Your Partisan Intensity Quotient (PIQ)   15
  What's Your State of Embattlement?   19

Chapter 2: Know Your Enemy   **23**
  The Conservative Manifesto   24
  Frequently Asked Questions
    about Conservatives   28
  A Field Guide to the Conservative Genus   35
  Other Conservative Species You
    May Encounter   41
  How to Rate a Conservative's Partisan
    Intensity Quotient (PIQ)   43
  A Glimpse into the Conservative Utopia   47

**Chapter 3: Can't We All
Just Get Along?**   **51**

A Day in the Life of
    Conservatives vs. Liberals   52

Battle of the Bumper Stickers   58

What Liberals Say vs.
    What Conservatives Hear   61

What Conservatives Say vs.
    What Liberals Hear   63

Common Enemies We Can
    All Agree to Hate   66

Chapter 4: Basic Training   **73**

The Seven Habits of Highly
    Ineffective Partisans   74

Do You Suffer from
    Argumentile Dysfunction?   78

How Not to Be an Asshole   82

The Ten Commandments
    of Partisan Warfare   87

How to Avoid Unhinged Lunatics   95

How to Detect Bullshit   98

How to Trip Up a Bullshitter   102

How to Spot Logical Fallacies   103

How to Win When You Can't
   Win Them Over   108

**Chapter 5: How to Win Friends While
Antagonizing People**   **111**
   How to Survive Family Sparring Matches   112
   What to Do If You're Sleeping
      with the Enemy   116
   How to Manage Workplace Squabbles   119
   How to Clash with Perfect Strangers   123
   How to Argue Politics on
      Facebook and Twitter   125
   How to Properly Engage
      in Internet Flame Wars   130

**Chapter 6: Kick-Ass Comebacks
to Conservative Nonsense**   **137**
   How to Argue with an Obamaphobe   138
   How to Argue with Economic Ignoramuses   143
   How to Taunt a Tea Partier   148
   How to Clash with Clueless
      Conservatives on Hot-Button Issues   153
   How to Argue with Bible-Thumpers   158
   How to Rebut Other Conservative Drivel   162

Chapter 7: The Conservative Hall of Shame   **169**

The Wing of Batshit Crazy   170

The Wing of Douche Bags   177

The Wing of Sex Fiends,
Perverts, and Adulterers   183

Chapter 8: How to Use Conservatives' Own Words against Them   **191**

Stunningly Moronic Conservative Quotes   192

Breathtakingly Delusional
Conservative Quotes   202

Shockingly Sociopathic
Conservative Quotes   212

After-*words*   **217**

When All Else Fails: 125,000 Ways
to Insult Conservatives   217

Acknowledgments   **221**

About the Author   **224**

Introduction

"Many are asking if our political discourse has gotten too heated. And those people should go to hell!"

—**Stephen Colbert**

S o you want to smack some sense into those clueless conservative morons (or "morans" as they would spell it). Good for you!

Was it your loudmouthed uncle's ridiculous rants about that "socialist Kenyan Nazi" in the White House that pushed you over the edge?

Was it those Tea Partiers parading around with their "Keep your government hands off my Medicare" signs that presented a clear and present danger to your sanity?

Or was it the mere ten seconds you accidentally spent watching Fox News that made you want to shout epithets and throw furniture at your TV?

All of the above?

You've heard all the conservative "arguments": Liberals are godless socialists who are fixing to bring Grandma before a death panel; liberals are pot-smoking Bible-bashers who are coming for your guns, your wallet, and your fetuses and will turn everyone gay; Obama is a tyrannical dictator who has done absolutely nothing *and* is destroying America.

Whether you're a liberal, progressive, Democrat, independent, or someone who's just tired of conservatives and their idiocy, chances are those righties have driven you mad as hell, and since you picked up this book, you probably can't take it anymore.

But if you're like most people, your past attempts at butting heads with conservatives have probably gone one of two ways: (1) you've tried reasoning with them, only to come away with that concussive feeling of banging your head against a wall of steel-reinforced ignorance; or (2) you've tried screaming at conservatives, only to make yourself hoarse while they go about their business of fouling the air and treading on the poor.

Either way, who could blame you if you've decided

that arguing with conservatives is a hopeless cause? You probably figure it's best simply to avoid them, just as you would a crazy person shouting at pigeons in the park (because sometimes it's better to leave Glenn Beck alone with his thoughts).

But unfortunately, that's part of the problem with political discourse in America today. Too many reasonable people shy away from debate and let their more determined and vocal right-wing rivals spew their nonsense with impunity. Left unchallenged, it then spreads like crabgrass across the political landscape. Soon it's everywhere—sprouting up at neighborhood barbecues, surrounding you at the office water cooler, or, when you're least expecting it, creeping into your Facebook news feed.

By continuing to stay silent, you let them win. That's why if you want to fight the right, you must stand up and speak truth to stupid.

We won't lie to you. Beating conservatives into submission is a tall order, especially in this political climate, with ignorance on the rise, reason on the decline, and right-wing douche-baggery at an all-time high.

It's hard to argue with fact-allergic, reality-impaired imbeciles who are fed a steady diet of misinformation and paranoid delusions from Fox News, right-wing radio squawkers, and loons like half-governor Sarah Palin and half-wit Michele Bachmann.

As Bill Maher put it, "Trying to get today's Republican to accept basic facts is like trying to get your dog to take a pill. You have to feed them the truth wrapped in a piece of baloney, hold their snout shut, and stroke their throats. And even then, just when you think they've swallowed it, they spit it out on the linoleum."

So what's an honest, conservative-loathing American to do?

The answer is to fight them with laughter. That's where this book comes in handy. We're not talking about turning political debate into a joke or making a mockery of serious issues. It's about learning how to wield humor as a weapon, cultivate your sense of irony, and sharpen your arguments with witty retorts. It's about learning to lighten things up as a way to maintain your own sanity and disarm your opponents.

Mark Twain once said, "The human race has one really effective weapon, and that is laughter." It's especially true in political debate. Just think of one of the most effective lines ever used in a presidential debate, when Ronald Reagan was asked during his 1984 face-off with Walter Mondale if his advanced age was a liability. "I want you to know that also I will not make age an issue of this campaign," Reagan said. "I am not going to exploit, for political purposes, my opponent's youth and inexperience."

In addition to helping you wage comedic warfare, this book also offers other handy tips that will help you outwit, out-mock, and outrage your conservative rivals. We will show you how to:

★　Learn basic rules of engagement, including how to frame arguments to your advantage, point out hypocrisy, and properly ridicule your opponents when necessary.

★　Explain why the Left is right and the Right is wrong with the dueling Conservative and Liberal Manifestos.

★　Throw winning comebacks at Tea Partiers, Bible-thumpers, economic ignoramuses, Obamaphobes, and other purveyors of conservative nonsense.

★　Determine if you suffer from argumentile dysfunction and, if so, learn how to avoid deadly pitfalls, such as promoting conspiracy theories, using Nazi analogies, or making the mistake of arguing with idiots.

★　Identify bullshit arguments, slice through Swiss-cheese logic, and expose fallacious reasoning.

★ Survive family sparring matches, manage work-place squabbles, and even learn to cope if you're sleeping with the enemy.

★ Entertain your friends and terrify your enemies while arguing politics on Facebook and Twitter.

★ Use conservatives' own words and deeds against them with the help of a handy guide to some of the most ridiculous, moronic, and laughable things today's conservative icons have said and done.

★ Should all else fail, hurl imaginative insults at your knuckle-dragging, mouth-breathing opponents by selecting from a handy cheat sheet containing 125,000 winning putdowns.

Politics was never meant to be a spectator sport. Political debate is simply too important to be left to the so-called experts in Washington and the media, who invariably just screw it up for the rest of us. That's why it falls on ordinary citizens like you to take the fight to the Right and defend America against every intolerant, corrupt, arrogant, greed-mongering, Fox News-parroting, Scripture-spouting, science-hating, reality-denying ideal for which they stand.

If you don't, the "morans" have already won.

★ CHAPTER 1 ★

What It Means to Be a Liberal

"Somebody came along and said 'liberal' means 'soft on crime, soft on drugs, soft on Communism, soft on defense, and we're gonna tax you back to the Stone Age because people shouldn't have to go to work if they don't want to.' And instead of saying, 'Well, excuse me, you right-wing, reactionary, xenophobic, homophobic, anti-education, anti-choice, pro-gun, Leave-It-to-Beaver trip back to the fifties,' we cowered in the corner and said, 'Please don't hurt me.'"

—NBC's *The West Wing*

No one can pinpoint the exact moment it happened, but sometime in the last thirty years—between Ronald Reagan's withering ridicule of all things liberal, George W. Bush's bullying crusade to stamp out dissent, and the Tea Party's demonization of the Left as enemies of liberty—conservatives gave liberalism a giant wedgie.

Liberalism never saw it coming. It was too busy flexing its muscles and gazing at its navel, when conservatives snuck up from behind, grabbed it by its tighty-whities, and hung it up on the flagpole. There, liberalism kicked and flailed, while conservatives got everybody to laugh and point. Then, to add insult to injury, they stole liberalism's girlfriend and lunch money.

Time was, liberalism was a word that conjured such core American principles as social justice, national compassion, and the rule of law. Democrats and even some Republicans used to wear the liberal label with pride. But then conservatives had an idea. What if liberalism could be turned into an embarrassing perversion, like pedophilia, or a disease, like leprosy?

And so they reinvented the word "liberal" as a catch-all expletive, a sort of shorthand way to describe spineless, godless, elitist, lazy, tie-dyed, pony-tailed, hemp-clad socialists.

To be honest, liberals have done a crappy job defending themselves in the face of this assault. They've countered by painting conservatives as heartless, bigoted, illiterate, inbred, unmedicated, homeschooled, backwoods hatemongers. Which, of course, is completely true. But liberals still struggle when it comes to standing up and defining their own core beliefs.

This is true for your average liberal on the street and the Democratic Party as a whole. Despite scoring some big victories, like President Obama's epic win in 2008, liberals have run into hard times trying to advance their values in the face of relentless conservative opposition. The fact is, liberals often get outmaneuvered by more aggressive and nimble partisans on the Right. As Jon Stewart once put it, "It's not that the Democrats are playing checkers and the Republicans are playing chess. It's that the Republicans are playing chess and the Democrats are in the nurse's office because once again they glued their balls to their thighs."

That's why, if liberals hope to be persuasive and start kicking some serious conservative ass, they need to stand tall, fight back, and confidently declare who they are and what they stand for. In short, they need to have some balls, preferably not glued to their thighs.

As a first step in girding for battle with conservatives,

it's essential to have a firm fix on your own beliefs. Take the following quiz to determine where you fit in the larger liberal mix.

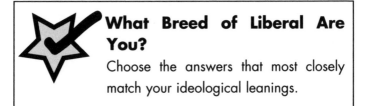

What Breed of Liberal Are You?

Choose the answers that most closely match your ideological leanings.

1. Which bumper sticker would you most likely put on your car?

_____A. Nice Hummer—Sorry About Your Penis

_____B. Democrats: Cleaning Up Republican Messes Since 1933

_____C. Jesus Was A Hippie

_____D. Abolish Corporate Personhood

_____E. Evolution Is Just A Theory…Kind Of Like Gravity

_____F. Honk If My Taxes Support Your Whiny Tea-bagging Ass

2. An asteroid is headed for Earth. You have a seat on the last shuttle off the planet. If you could bring only one book with which to build a future civilization, what would it be?

_____A. *An Inconvenient Truth*, by Al Gore

_____ B. *The Hitchhiker's Guide to the Galaxy*, by Douglas Adams

_____ C. *The Courage to Survive*, by Dennis Kucinich

_____ D. *A People's History of the United States*, by Howard Zinn

_____ E. *The Origin of Species*, by Charles Darwin

_____ F. *I Am America (And So Can You!)*, by Stephen Colbert

3. A second civil war has just broken out in America. Who is to blame?

_____ A. Global warming deniers—for continuing to reject reality despite rising oceans off the coast of Kansas

_____ B. Bible-thumping puritans—for attempting to ban abortion, gay people, and sex

_____ C. Rick Perry—for actually seceding Texas from the Union and legalizing the hunting of humans for sport/capital punishment/reality TV

_____ D. Corporate America—for attempting to buy naming rights to the Exxon Mobil/Goldman Sachs/Wal-Mart States of America

_____ E. Fox News—for promoting a "fair and balanced" overthrow of the government with a flashy "March to Civil War" logo and theme music

_____F. Sarah Palin—for her "Civil War in America" bus tour, where she raised an army of mindless followers, led them across a bridge to nowhere, and then quit halfway through

4. If the Founding Fathers were alive today, they would be most appalled by which of the following?
_____A. That hemp is illegal. Come on, what wasn't clear about the "pursuit of happiness"?
_____B. That people think guys who wore powdered wigs and Capri pants were against gay marriage
_____C. The military-industrial-evangelical complex
_____D. That the Bush-packed Supreme Court thinks corporations are people too
_____E. That today's Tea Party is the total opposite of their Tea Party
_____F. That sixty million people punched ballots with Sarah Palin's name on it in '08

5. If you could time-travel back to any historical event and bring one thing with you, what would you choose?
_____A. The day BP began spilling oil into the Gulf of Mexico—with a giant ShamWow
_____B. The day the Supreme Court anointed George W. Bush president—with a video montage

recapping the disasters of 9/11, two botched wars, Katrina, and the financial collapse

_____C. The 1967 Summer of Love—with a truckload of condoms

_____D. The day Monica Lewinsky brought Bill Clinton pizza—with a dry-cleaning coupon

_____E. Honolulu, Hawaii, August 4, 1961—with a video camera to capture Obama's birth on film and shut the birthers up once and for all

_____F. The day that Dick Cheney was first seduced by the Dark Side of the Force—with a lightsaber

6. If you were a candidate for political office, what would your theme song be?

_____A. "It's Not Easy Being Green," by Kermit the Frog

_____B. "Fight the Power," by Public Enemy

_____C. "Let Them Eat War," by Bad Religion

_____D. "Take This Job and Shove It," by Johnny Paycheck

_____E. "I Still Haven't Found What I'm Looking For," by U2

_____F. "It's the End of the World as We Know It (And I Feel Fine)," by R.E.M.

7. Which of the following groupings of people would you most like to see brought before a death panel, and on what charges?

_____A. The CEOs of BP, Exxon Mobil, and Chevron—for fouling our air, poisoning our oceans, and melting our ice caps

_____B. Justices Roberts, Scalia, Thomas, and Alito—for working to roll back most of the social progress achieved over the last century

_____C. George H. W. Bush, George W. Bush, and Jeb Bush—for past and future crimes against humanity

_____D. Wall Street bankers—for turning the stock market into a rigged casino and robbing us blind

_____E. Sarah Palin, Michele Bachmann, and Glenn Beck—for being ignorant douche bags and lying to other ignorant douche bags

_____F. Rick Perry, cancer, and cigarettes—for sending more people to the grave than a death panel

8. What region of the country would you most like to see kicked out of the Union?

_____A. Texas—execution-happy breeding ground for idiot presidents and fossil fools

_____B. The South—home to Civil War-reenacting knuckle-draggers and Confederate flag-waving bigots

_____C. NASCAR country—home to chest-thumping, flag-waving jingoists and beer-swilling yahoos

_____D. Wall Street—home to greed-mongering, Ponzi-scheming white collar crooks

_____E. The Bible Belt—home to Rapture-ready, God-misappropriating evangeliclowns

_____F. Arizona—home to gun-toting racists and rogue cops itching to racially profile anyone who's a shade south of white, as well as really old people who drive slow and won't get out of the fast lane

9. If you could chisel any Americans, living or dead, onto Mt. Rushmore, who would you choose?

_____A. Al Gore, Robert Kennedy Jr., John Muir, and a giant compact fluorescent light bulb

_____B. Cesar Chavez, Rosa Parks, Harvey Milk, and Angelina Jolie

_____C. Martin Luther King Jr., Bob Dylan, Michael Moore, and George Clooney

_____D. Bill, Hillary, Barack, and Oprah

_____E. Keith Olbermann, Rachel Maddow, Al Franken, and "President" Martin Sheen

_____F. Jon Stewart, Stephen Colbert, Bill Maher, and Conan O'Brien

Scoring

If you answered mostly A's, you're an *Eco-Avenger*, also known as an environmentalist or tree hugger. You believe in saving the planet from the clutches of air-fouling, oil-drilling, earth-raping conservative fossil fools.

If you answered mostly B's, you're a *Social Justice Crusader*, also known as a rights activist. You believe in equality, fairness, and preventing neo-Confederate conservative troglodytes from rolling back fifty years of civil rights gains.

If you answered mostly C's, you're a *Peace Patroller*, also known as an anti-war liberal or neo-hippie. You believe in putting an end to American imperial conquest, stopping wars that have already been lost, and supporting our troops by bringing them home.

If you answered mostly D's, you're a *Working Class Warrior*, also known as an Occupier and a blue-collar Democrat. You believe that the little guy is getting screwed by conservative greed-mongers and corporate criminals, and you're not going to take it anymore.

If you answered mostly E's, you're a *Reality-Based Intellectualist*, also known as a liberal elitist. You are a proud member of what's known as the reality-based community, where science, reason, and non-Jesus-centric thought reign supreme.

If you answered mostly F's, you're a *New Left Hipster*, also known as a MoveOn.org liberal, Netroots activist, or *Daily Show* fanatic. You believe that if we really want to defend American values, conservative hatriots must be exposed and mocked for every fanatical, puritanical, soulless, paranoid, fact-free, obstructionist ideal for which they stand.

If your answers don't match any of the above, that means you're a label-defying iconoclast or a hybrid of various types. Consider it a point of pride.

If manual scoring is too antiquated for your tastes, you can take an online version of this quiz at www.FightConservatives. com, where you can also share your results with a friend.

"*If you don't stand for anything, you don't stand for anything!*"

—George W. Bush

As you can see, liberals are a diverse breed. But there is a core set of values and common causes that unites them all. Since it's important to have a clear idea of your world view before you engage conservatives and go about the business of destroying theirs, we present...

The Liberal Manifesto

Liberals believe that fighting for social justice, equal rights, a social safety net, and economic justice for the 99% is for the common good, and not part of a socialist plot.

Liberals believe that clean air, clean water, access to education, and universal health care are basic human rights, not privileges—and seriously not part of a socialist plot.

Liberals believe in getting their news from Jon Stewart and their comedy from Fox News.

Liberals refuse to believe that corporations are people until Texas executes one.

Liberals believe in two simple things that will save the economy: gay bridal registries and taxing legalized marijuana.

Liberals believe in separating church and hate and doing what Jesus would actually do, instead of lobbying for more tax cuts that benefit the wealthy, while stripping food stamps away from the poor.

Liberals believe that just because you're rich, you're not a "job creator," particularly if your name is Snooki, and especially if you're a soulless CEO who has just laid off his entire U.S. work force because he found a Chinese sweatshop that can do the work on the cheap. That makes you a "job exporter," and a douche bag.

Liberals believe in the supremacy of science, facts, and reason-based thought, and that if global warming and evolution are theories, then so are gravity and NASCAR.

Liberals believe in offering conservatives a concession: don't pray in our schools, and we won't think in your churches.

Liberals believe there is no bigger government than the one that listens to your phone calls for your own protection, wants to put itself in charge of every single pregnancy, censors your textbooks, arrests and detains you indefinitely without charge, or attempts to dictate who you can marry.

Liberals believe the best way to fight terror is to hunt down and kill the terrorists that actually attacked you. Mission accomplished! You're welcome!

Liberals believe that supporting our troops doesn't

just mean wearing American-flag underwear; it means not sending soldiers off to fight phony wars in the first place, and not voting people into office who plan to slash veterans' benefits to spite the other party. (Republicans, we're looking at you.)

Liberals believe that no banks are too big to fail, too big to be held to stricter financial regulations, or too big to have the people running them thrown in jail for ripping America off.

Liberals believe that deep-pocketed special interests shouldn't be allowed to spend unlimited money to buy off politicians and game our elections because when private power becomes stronger than the state itself, that's what Franklin Roosevelt once called the essence of fascism. Or as Republicans call it, a fund-raiser.

And more than anything else, liberals believe that it's time to come together as a country, restore sanity, and refuse to be held hostage by a merry band of right-wing faux patriots who stand for blocking or repealing all of the above and turning American into a corpo-fascist idiocracy that's for sale to the highest bidder.

Rate Your Partisan Intensity Quotient (PIQ)

Beyond basic ideology, we also need to assess your partisan temperament. Are you the type of person who eagerly engages conservatives in debate or do you avoid confrontation at all costs? Answer the following questions, and we'll rate your PIQ.

1. Your neighbor has just placed a very large Mitt Romney 2012 sign on her lawn. Which of the following would you do?

_____A. Show respect for her right to free speech

_____B. Put up an even larger Obama 2012 sign

_____C. Graffiti her sign in the middle of the night by writing "Sucks" underneath "Romney"

_____D. Graffiti your own Obama 2012 sign and then publicly accuse her of defacing your property

2. Your coworker is complaining to anyone in earshot that his health-care premiums went up because of "Obamacare." Which of the following would you do?

_____A. Remind him that health-care companies set rates, not the government

_____B. Point out that his rates might be lower if he

weighed less than 400 pounds and didn't break into a sweat just from breathing

_____C. Advise him he's three weeks behind on quota and he's going to be glad he'll have coverage when he's canned

_____D. Give him a chance to experience the healthcare system firsthand when you hit him in the face with a stapler

3. You're at an "Occupy" protest, when a Republican heckler appears out of nowhere and begins chanting "Occupy a job!" while hoisting a sign that says "These protests are making it difficult to get to my yacht." Which of the following would you do?

_____A. Embrace him in the spirit of tolerance and respect for diversity

_____B. Hoist up your "BBQ the Rich" sign and drown him out with your own "We are the 99%" chant

_____C. Occupy his mouth with a roll of duct tape

_____D. Wrestle him to the ground and smack him repeatedly with your "Tolerance is a two-way street" sign

4. You run into John Boehner at a tanning salon. Which of the following would you do?

_____A. Ask him how he likes getting the deluxe package. Apologize for making him cry.

_____B. Tell him you don't think it's appropriate for him to have his tanning paid for by his government-run health plan. Apologize for making him cry.

_____C. Tell him he looks like the world's saddest tangerine. Eventually apologize for making him cry.

_____D. Tell him that whenever anyone sees his name in writing, they read it "boner" in their heads because he's a dick. Let him cry.

5. You're at a family BBQ and your Tea Party brother-in-law starts ranting about the trillions of dollars Obama has added to the deficit. Which of the following would you do?

_____A. Play _Angry Birds_ on your iPhone to take out your aggressions

_____B. Say a quiet prayer that your sister gets divorced

_____C. Correct him by saying that the majority of the deficit is fueled by Bush's wars and tax cuts

_____D. Gently remind him that the deficit wouldn't be so high if he wasn't using his unemployment checks to gas up his jet ski

6. You're at your daughter's school, and the chair of the PTA is demanding that evolution be removed from the curriculum and replaced with intelligent design. Which of the following would you do?

_____A. Suggest that perhaps intelligent design could be mentioned as an alternate theory to evolution

_____B. Pillage your retirement and enroll your daughter in a private school

_____C. Point out his large suborbital ridges and his striking resemblance to a great ape

_____D. Tell her "sure," as long as she can show you the part in the Bible that mentions dinosaurs

Scoring Your PIQ

Award yourself zero points for every A, one point for every B, two points for every C, and three points for every D.

15–18: Severe ☆☆☆☆☆☆☆☆☆☆☆☆☆☆☆☆☆☆

You're a _Flame-Throwing Revolutionary_: There's a waterboard and an "enemy combatant" label in your future, and it may help if you're not allergic to tear gas.

11–14: High ☆☆☆☆☆☆☆☆☆☆☆☆☆

You're a _Fierce Fighter._ You will argue politics any time

and any place, which makes you unpopular at funerals, weddings, and baby showers.

7–10: Elevated ★★★★★★★

You're a *Passionate Foot Soldier*. You stand up for what you believe in, but odds are, like most people, you'll bail out of an argument if things get heated.

3–6: Guarded ★★★★

You're a *Casual Observer*. You speak up when you feel it's safe, but not if it conflicts with *Modern Family*.

0–2: Low ★

You're a *Noncombatant*. You're like the French of political discourse, waving the white flag at the slightest sign of resistance. Time to grow a pair.

What's Your State of Embattlement?

Everyone is familiar with the much-ballyhooed red vs. blue divide, which separates America into Republican and Democratic states. But that obviously doesn't tell the whole story, as no state is uniformly red or blue. You've heard of other regional divides like the Bible

Belt and the Rust Belt, but there are many other "belts" that describe partisan America. To determine your State of Embattlement, locate the belt below that most closely corresponds to your specific locality.

THE BELTS OF RED AMERICA

If you are a liberal living in...

The Chastity Belt (southern and middle America, where abstinence pledges are almost as high as the teenage birthrates)

The Dow Jones Belt (where the belts they wear cost more than your house)

The Megachurch Belt (where come-as-you-are churches have grown so large they have their own zip codes)

The Locked-and-Loaded Belt (shoot-first, ask-no-questions-later country)

The Caviar-and-Cocaine Belt (home to the old-money, country-club set)

The Border Belt (the front lines of an imaginary immigration war)

...you are *Desperately Besieged*. You're surrounded by so many conservatives, it's like being the last person left at the end of a zombie movie. Arguing with them seems like a lost cause, and the best you can do is lay low and hide, lest they suck out your brain and turn you into one of them. Remember the shoot-out at the end of *Butch Cassidy and the Sundance Kid?* That's pretty much what you're looking at.

THE BELTS OF PURPLE AMERICA

If you are a liberal living in...

The Blue Collar Belt (communities divided between old-guard labor and people too stupid to recognize they are voting against their own economic interests)

The Cookie-Cutter Belt (middle-class planned communities where you can't tell your house from your neighbor's house, also known as Oxycontin Country)

The Can't-Buckle-My-Belt (where fatties are furious over the shrinking American pie and the fact that it's not all-you-can-eat)

The Slot-Jockey Belt (casino country, where smoking, booze, and one-armed bandits rule the land, e.g., Nevada, Atlantic City, Mississippi River Valley)

The Stroke Belt (retirement communities from Florida to Arizona, overrun by silver foxes)

The Meth Belt (where rolling meth labs keep the burbs humming and dentists in business)

...you are *Battle-Hardened*. You have so many fights you want to pick with the conservatives all around you that you may not even know where to start. Sleep with one eye open and make sure you know who your friends are.

THE BELTS OF BLUE AMERICA

If you are a liberal living in...

The Born-This-Way Belt (enclaves of America that are fabulously gay)

The Bagel Belt (urban areas with a high concentration of equal parts wisecracking and complaining Jews: "You call this soup hot? Feh!")

The Botox Belt (the land of high cheekbones, fake boobs, and liposuctioned fannies, from Hollywood to Manhattan)

The Ivory-Tower Belt (cocoons dominated by intellectual and academic elites)

The Tofurky Belt (the land of militant vegans and hairy, naked tree huggers)

The Bong Belt (stoner country, where the munchies dictate day-to-day activities)

...you are *Safely Entrenched*. You're surrounded by so many people who agree with you that your arguing skills may have gone flabby from disuse. Be careful not to injure your neck from nodding in agreement.

Whatever situation you find yourself in, your goal is the same: engage your enemies wherever they lurk. But first you must understand your enemy...

★ **CHAPTER 2** ★

Know Your Enemy

"If you know the enemy and know yourself, you need not fear the result of a hundred battles. If you know yourself but not the enemy, for every victory gained you will also suffer a defeat."

—Sun Tzu, *The Art of War*

Before you engage conservatives in combat, it's important to have a clear understanding of exactly who your enemies are, including their core beliefs, specific ideological profile, and vision for America. Doing so will enable you to better dissect, ridicule, and exploit their weaknesses for maximum advantage.

For starters, here's a look at what conservatives truly stand for:

The Conservative Manifesto

Conservatives believe in tax favors for the rich, tax hikes on the poor, dumb kids, smart bombs, and that what's good for Wal-Mart and Exxon Mobil is good for America.

Conservatives believe in wrapping themselves in the Confederate flag, burning the social safety net so it pollutes the air, and repealing the entire twentieth century.

Conservatives believe in government of, by, and for the wealthiest 1% and that if the 99% don't like that, they can buy off their own politicians or go suck it.

Conservatives believe in serving tea steeped in prejudice, fear, anger, bitterness, paranoia, intolerance, jingoism, cynicism, hypocrisy, and selfishness, and calling it a party.

Conservatives believe pizza is a vegetable, pepper spray is a food product, mustard gas is a condiment, and bamboo under the fingernails is a manicure.

Conservatives believe in "clean" coal befouling spacious skies, amber waves of abstinent teens, and purple mountains of middle-class debt.

Conservatives believe that public education is just another entitlement that needs to be cut.

Conservatives believe in tightening eligibility for unemployment benefits, welfare, and food stamps, while loosening gun control laws, because what we really need are more desperate, jobless people with access to guns.

Conservatives believe corporations are people, all rich people are automatically "job creators," women who use contraception are sluts, the gay can be prayed away, poor people deserve to be poor because it's their own damn fault, the Girl Scouts have a secret lesbian agenda, global warming is a hoax, the Bible trumps the Constitution, Donald Trump trumps the Bible, Fox News is actually "fair and balanced," the U.S. president is a Muslim sleeper agent from Kenya, and conservatives are the ones who understand the "real world."

Conservatives believe John Boehner's tears will trickle down and stimulate the economy.

Conservatives believe that if historical reality doesn't fit your preferred narrative, you simply edit Wikipedia to suit your propagandistic needs.

Conservatives believe in cutting social services while giving multi-million-dollar tax subsidies to Bible-themed amusement parks, because it's more important to take your child to see Jesus ride an animatronics dinosaur than to be able to treat her Type 1 diabetes.

Conservatives believe in shipping jobs overseas—except for CEOs, lobbyists, Starbucks baristas, and their own illegal nannies.

Conservatives believe in weapons of mass deception, bought elections, and pharmaceutical erections.

Conservatives believe they've just seen an apparition of the Virgin Mary in a grilled cheese sandwich and a vision of Jesus in Herman Cain's pizza.

Conservatives believe America was a better place when there were Hummers on the street, Bushes in office, Jack Bauer in prime time, prayer in schools, abortions in back alleys, gays in the closet, segregation on buses, and only white male property owners could vote.

Conservatives believe in proclaiming themselves pro-life until you pass through the birth canal, at which point they become pro-"go screw yourself," and couldn't care less if you don't have health insurance, can't feed your family, or get executed for a crime you didn't commit.

Conservatives believe in proclaiming that they steadfastly and unflinchingly support our troops, as long as they're not gay.

Conservatives believe that abstinence-only education has worked so well for their pregnant unwed teenage daughters that it should be replicated all across the nation.

Conservatives believe that anything liberals believe must necessarily be false, which is why they believe that low-flow toilets and energy efficient light bulbs pose a bigger threat to our way of life than melting ice caps.

Conservatives believe in stoking fears about

government death panels, and then cheering the idea of letting uninsured patients die, because they clearly have no idea what irony means.

Conservatives believe in railing against the estate tax, even if they're living in trailers.

Conservatives believe in the kind of ass-backward logic that says even though 9/11 happened under George W. Bush's watch, it was Bill Clinton's fault, and even though Barack Obama was the one who ordered Osama bin Laden killed, Bush deserves the credit.

Conservatives believe that electrified fences and Taser guns should be considered comprehensive immigration reform.

Conservatives believe in abolishing the Department of Education and cutting school funding because it's a known fact that uneducated simpletons are more likely to grow up and vote Republican.

And more than anything else, conservatives believe that no matter how big an economic calamity you create, how big a hole you blow through the deficit, how badly you botch wars, or how drunk you were on trickled-down Kool-Aid when you drove the country into a ditch, everything is still Obama's fault.

"A conservative is a man with two perfectly good legs who, however, has never learned how to walk forward."

—Franklin Roosevelt

Frequently Asked Questions about Conservatives

Now that you know what you're up against, it's time to get to the vexing questions about conservatives' peculiar behavior and seemingly inexplicable belief system.

Q. How does someone become a conservative anyway?

A. Generally speaking, it starts with sexual frustration, blossoms into anger, and pretty soon you want to cut taxes.

Q. Why are conservatives so mean-spirited?

A. Because wealthy, white, Christian males are tired of living in a society where all the breaks go to poor, gay, illegal immigrants.

Q. Why are Republicans so angry about poor people in particular?

A. Conservatives are sick and tired of the lazy poor leeching their tax dollars. The wealthy work hard to collect their dividend checks and capital gains distributions. All that envelope-opening can really wear on you. The last thing they need is for some guy with three minimum-wage jobs asking for a handout. He already has three jobs! He's just being greedy. A Gulfstream jet goes for about $60 million! You'd be angry too if someone was trying to take your plane so his kids could have entitlements like food.

Q. How can conservatives possibly believe the lies and bullshit they're spoon-fed by Fox News and right-wing radio? Do they have any concept of reality?

A. As Stephen Colbert once observed, "Reality has a well-known liberal bias."

Q. Why are Republicans so inept at governing?

A. What did you expect from a party built around the idea that government doesn't work? The whole point of their policies is to create disasters so that when they get voted out, they can blame Democrats for failing to fix them, and then try to convince voters to put Republicans back in charge. That's what you do when you don't have any good ideas. To quote Bill Maher, "It's like a guy throwing shit on you and then selling you relief from the flies."

Q. Why are conservatives so fanatically obsessed with cutting taxes and spending, even when it's clear that neither has helped the economy? Do they just want to get rid of government?

A. As Grover Norquist, one of the most revered and feared right-wing power brokers, one said, "I don't want to abolish government. I simply want to reduce it to the size where I can drag it into the bathroom and drown it in the bathtub." So you see, they don't cut taxes and spending because they want to get rid of government. They do it because they're sociopaths.

Q. Why do so many staunchly anti-gay conservatives turn out to be secretly gay themselves?

A. Conservatives believe "Thou shalt not lie with mankind, as with womankind: it is abomination" (Leviticus 18:22). It's perfectly clear that God doesn't like gay sex to be had lying down. So if you must have gay sex, do it the Republican way: in an airport bathroom with a drunken underage staffer.

Q. What's with all the Nazi comparisons conservatives constantly make? Where do they get off calling Obama Hitler?

A. Psychologists call this projection.

Q. What are birthers?

A. These are the unhinged lunatics, crazy-haired real estate moguls, and Texas governors who, despite all evidence, still believe Obama was born in Kenya and that his birth certificate was forged as part of an elaborate conspiracy that began in 1961. These are the same people who believe the moon landing was staged on a movie lot in Hollywood and wear tinfoil hats so aliens can't steal their thoughts. Undaunted by the long-form birth certificate Obama produced, "These people," Jimmy Kimmel noted, "could have personally witnessed him being born out of an apple pie, in the middle of a Kansas wheat field, while Toby Keith sang the National Anthem—and they'd still think Obama was a Kenyan Muslim."

Q. What is the Tea Party anyway, and how are they different from the Republican Party?

A. The Tea Party isn't actually a real party. It's just a rebranding gimmick for Republican assholes. Contrary to popular myth, it didn't start as a populist grassroots uprising of newly awakened patriots. No, a bunch of deep-pocketed right-wing corporate puppet masters got together and said, "Hey, what if we took all the fundamentalists, racists, xenophobes, homophobes, Bible-bangers, latter-day Klansmen, Birch Society members, and flat-earthers who are always embarrassing us, and what if we dress them in tricornered hats, bankroll their hate-ins, and call it a party? They'll make us look positively sane by comparison." And so the Tea Party was born.

Q. Why are conservatives constantly trying to slash public education?

A. Conservatives say that since the country is broke, we can't afford to subsidize the underfunded schools that are failing our youth. So the best way to get rid of underfunded schools is to stop funding them. Problem solved. And while liberals see the youth of today as illiterate, uneducated, and unprepared for a complex world, conservatives see them as future Tea Party voters.

Q. Why do conservatives keep pushing the same supply side/voodoo economics policies that have been discredited?

A. Critics say these policies have crippled the middle class and have greatly increased the disparity between rich and poor. Failure? They crippled the middle class and have greatly increased the disparity between rich and poor. Mission accomplished. They are working exactly as planned.

Q. Are there any government jobs Republicans support?

A. Yes, Republicans are fully in favor of jobs for Republican politicians and also executioners. Everyone else is expendable.

Q. Why are conservatives so against women's reproductive rights?

A. Conservatives believe in small government—a government so small, it can fit in a uterus and prevent women from making decisions regarding their own lives. They believe a fetus has rights, especially Second Amendment rights. So until we can find a way to arm a fetus, someone has to step in and protect the innocent.

Q. When conservatives are in power, they seem to love the idea of stifling free thought, cracking down on civil liberties, and empowering a Big Brother-style authoritarian government. Didn't they ever read George Orwell's *1984*?

A. Yes, they just thought it was a how-to manual.

Q. Is there a covert conspiracy among oil interests, Republican power brokers, and the military industrial complex to wage a war for global domination and control of the world's oil reserves?

A. No, they're fairly open about it.

Q. If Jesus preached peace, why are so many Bible-thumping Christians so gung-ho about war?

A. According to Christian apocalypticism, war in the Middle East will lead to Armageddon, which will lead to an epic battle between the antichrist and Jesus, after which will come one thousand years of peace and plenty. So as you can see, it's actually a well-thought-out plan.

Q. Why are Republicans so disrespectful to Obama?

A. President Obama started it when he had the gall to run for president as the leader of the opposition party. Obama ran on a platform of hope and change, insinuating that America under Republican leadership was hopeless and in need of repair. That's pretty rude. How would you like it if someone came to your office, criticized your performance, and took your job? And what if he were younger, smarter, and better looking than you? That would hurt a little, wouldn't it?

Q. How likely is it that I will be shot by an armed Republican?

A. Unless you are driving a hybrid car through the South with bumper stickers that say "Yes we can again," "amnesty for illegals," "Just gay married," or "I've come to liberate you from your guns," it's fairly unlikely.

Q. How do conservatives sleep at night?

A. Like babies, actually, snuggly wrapped in a flag, on big bags of money, and comforted by the knowledge that someone else is fighting their wars of global conquest.

"Never underestimate the power of stupid people in large groups."

—**Anonymous**

A Field Guide to the Conservative Genus

Now it's time for you to meet the various species that make up the Republican Party's so-called "big tent." Familiarize yourself with the following handy field guide so that you can quickly size up your opponent.

RAPTUREFARIANS

Religious fundamentalists and Christian evangelicals eagerly awaiting the Rapture and the End Times so that they may ascend to heaven and leave all godless, liberal heathens behind

A.k.a.: Bible-thumpers, Christian Taliban, hypochristians, Rapture Right

Natural habitat: Applebee's

Turn-ons: School prayer, megachurches, Middle East holy wars, forcibly inserting feeding tubes into vegetative patients

Turn-offs: Evolution, stem cells, abortion clinics, secular judges, watching gay newlyweds kiss

Likely to be seen: Passing out "True Love Waits" virginity pledge cards to teens in front of Wet Seal at the local mall

Would sooner be caught dead than: Acknowledging the fact that teens who take abstinence pledges are five times more likely to engage in other non-biblically-sanctioned sex acts

GOLDMAN SACHTARIANS

Conservative über capitalists and apologists for big businesses who believe that trickle-down economics works wonders, job outsourcing is good for America, and large-scale fraud is simply an "accounting innovation"

A.k.a.: One percenters, country club Republicans, corporate criminals

Natural habitat: Wall Street, K Street, minimum security jails

Turn-ons: The magic of the market (i.e., offshore tax shelters, no-bid contracts, and cheap, illegal immigrant labor)

Turn-offs: Welfare recipients, labor unions, trial lawyers, congressional subpoenas

Likely to be seen: Hiring a guy named "Bob" in Bangalore, India, to do your old job for half the cost

Would sooner be caught dead than: Actually paying taxes

TEATARDS

Radical right-wing faux patriots who believe in low taxes and an extremely limited federal government (especially when the president is a socialist Kenyan black guy); are known for their loud and angry protests unwittingly on the behalf of persecuted minorities like multinational corporations and billionaires

A.k.a.: Get-off-my-lawners, Obstructionist Americans, Congress

Natural habitat: Anywhere the Koch brothers bus them to (*see Chapter 7: The Conservative Hall of Shame*

if you're not acquainted with the Tea Party's corporate overlords, David and Charles Koch)

Turn-ons: Hockey moms, low taxes, holding America hostage and threatening cataclysmic default when they don't get their way

Turn-offs: Obama, Obamacare, Michelle Obama, Bo Obama

Likely to be seen: Painting Hitler mustaches on Obama posters

Would sooner be caught dead than: Protesting wars, Wall Street, disproportionately low taxes on billionaires, or any other component of the deficit that doesn't punish poor people

HATRIOTS

Militant, chest-pounding patrio-fascists who believe war is peace, freedom is slavery, ignorance is strength, and two plus two equals whatever Glenn Beck says it does

A.k.a.: Digital brownshirts, chicken hawks, keyboard commandos

Natural habitat: Talk-radio airwaves, online forums trolled by like-minded bottom-feeders, GOP congressional leadership

Turn-ons: The Patriot Act, groupthink, issuing anonymous death threats to liberal bloggers

Turn-offs: Free speech, logic, reason

Likely to be seen: Monitoring their grandmother's library records for signs of subversive activity

Would sooner be caught dead than: Actually serving in the military

GUNFEDERATES

Rednecks with Confederate flags on their pickup trucks; known to carry concealed weapons as a last line of defense against liberal intellectuals and other would-be terrorists from the Northeast

A.k.a.: Angry white men, rednecks, anti-Washington conservatives

Natural habitat: Rural backwaters, trailer parks, and Ultimate Fighting Championship events everywhere

Turn-ons: *Guns & Ammo*, televised fishing, Civil War reenactments where the South wins

Turn-offs: Trigger locks and waiting periods

Likely to be seen: Stockpiling armaments to defend their Second Amendment rights in the event that one of the most gun-friendly Democratic presidents in history has a sudden change of heart

Would sooner be caught dead than: Defending the rest of the Bill of Rights

KOCH-HEADS

A shameless group of greedy mega-rich business interests who take their cues from the Koch brothers and use their extravagant wealth to buy elections, politicians, and public opinion so they can increase their extravagant wealth, regardless of whom they screw, maim, or kill in the process

A.k.a.: Robber barons, capitalist pigs, trust-fund conservatives

Natural habitat: Smoke-filled rooms, Mr. Burns's mansion

Turn-ons: Raping the environment, crushing labor unions, undermining civil rights, doing business with Iran

Turn-offs: The middle class, the EPA, democracy

Likely to be seen: Funneling gobs of money to right-wing attack groups like Americans for Prosperity

Would sooner be caught dead than: Drinking the poisoned water or breathing the toxic air their factories spew

CHAZBONO-PHOBES

Social conservatives on the front lines of the culture wars who are fiercely committed to fighting the liberal/gay agenda; characterized by an all-consuming fear that a high-profile transgender man is a bigger threat to our nation's sexual security than an insanely popular television show dedicated to ballroom dancing

A.k.a.: Traditional-values voters, culture warriors, white-breads

Natural habitat: Suburbs and exurbs containing at least a 20:1 ratio of white Christians to ethnic and/or gay minorities

Turn-ons: Gay marriage bans, anti-sodomy laws

Turn-offs: Hollywood, exposed nipples (except Nancy Grace's), sex acts not explicitly endorsed by Pat Robertson

Likely to be seen: In Marcus Bachmann's "pray away the gay" clinic to cure them of their homoerotic thoughts

Would sooner be caught dead than: Within a 100-mile radius of San Francisco

Other Conservative Species You May Encounter

GRIDLOCKERS

A small but growing subspecies of teatards who would rather send the country into an apocalypse than allow the other side anything that could be perceived as even the smallest of victories. This group believes the federal government is failing and they are doing everything they can to help it get there.

UN-SCIENCE-TOLOGISTS

Proud ignoramuses who believe the science just isn't in yet on climate change, evolution, the dangers of smoking, gravity, and that whole "Round Earth Thing."

CORPOR-AVIDUALS

A flourishing species that believes corporations are people and would be proud if their daughter married one.

ELECTROCUNICIANS

A.k.a. fearless fryers, capital punishers, and the governor of Texas, this species is committed to carrying out capital punishment as often as possible, regardless of whether the convicted is underage, developmentally challenged, or innocent.

FOX TROTTERS

Smug, insufferable, true-believing conservatives who mindlessly parrot Fox News talking points under the misguided impression that they are fair-minded and chemically balanced.

BORN-AGAIN DEFICIT HATERS

Until January 2009, the federal deficit didn't matter to this subspecies of Teatard, but once conservatives were out of office, it became a big deal that needed to be dealt with at any cost, unless of course it required raising taxes on billionaires.

NASCARCISSISTS

Slack-jawed, beer-soaked yahoos who derive as much endless amusement from taunting spineless liberal pansies as they do from watching cars drive around in circles.

"Hell is other people."

—Jean-Paul Sartre

How to Rate a Conservative's Partisan Intensity Quotient (PIQ)

In addition to being familiar with various conservative species, you will also need to gauge the extent of your opponent's partisan passion, inflexibility, or possible pathology. You can quickly determine your opponent's PIQ with this simple test. Award one point for each "yes" answer.

_____1. Have they tattooed the Second Amendment, "We the people," "Don't Tread on Me," or "Mega Dittos" anywhere on their person?

_____2. Are their children homeschooled because they believe public education is a "homosexual Ponzi scheme"?

_____3. Do their calendars include events like Civil War reenactments, fantasy NASCAR drafts, Ayn Rand's birthday, or book burnings?

_____4. When you look at their Facebook profiles, do their interests include racial profiling, phone tapping, or waterboarding?

_____5. Do their iPod playlists alternate between Glenn Beck podcasts, Toby Keith, and Wagner?

_____6. Do they prefer the Koch brothers to the Blues Brothers, Coen brothers, or Doobie Brothers?

_____7. Do they own a copy of *Mein Kampf, The Protocols of the Elders of Zion*, or anything written by Ann Coulter?

_____8. Are they so concerned about immigration that they build an electrified fence around Taco Bell?

_____9. Have they ever tweeted "OMG Just ran into Mama Grizzly tour bus somebody pinch me"?

_____10. Do they regularly rant about Obamacare in the comments section of Internet news articles, even if the article is titled "This Fall's Hottest Fashions!"?

____11. Are they a member of the "Gun-of-the-Month Club"?

____12. Do they believe 9/11, Hurricane Katrina, and the BP oil spill are God's wrath over gays, hip-hop music, and Hollywood?

____13. Do they blame state deficits on greedy teachers, municipal trash collectors, and money-grubbing cops and firemen?

____14. Do they hate walks in baseball because they view it as socialist welfare?

____15. Do they talk about the Founding Fathers more than their own fathers?

____16. Do they refer to Ronald Reagan as a Founding Father?

____17. Do they constantly confuse our Constitution with their Bible?

____18. Do they believe a woman's right to choose is whether she has her baby at a home or in a hospital?

____19. Are they convinced that Fox News has a liberal bias?

____20. Do they frequently blame Obama for things like inclement weather, the Yankees' losing streak, or their own erectile dysfunction?

SCORING

16–20: SEVERE

Your opponent is an *Unhinged Extremist* (and likely armed). Approach with extreme caution.

12–15: HIGH

Your opponent is a *Pugnacious Pitbull*. Nothing short of an absolute beat-down will give them pause for thought.

8–11: ELEVATED

Your opponent is a *Dedicated Disciple*. Wear a hard hat and pack a lunch.

4–7: GUARDED

Your opponent is a *Casual Combatant*. Overwhelm them with shock and awe.

0–3: LOW

Your opponent is a *Guaranteed Pushover*. This guy should fall faster than John Boehner's approval ratings.

"The party of Lincoln and Liberty was transmogrified into the party of hairy-backed swamp developers and corporate shills, faith-based economists, fundamentalist bullies with Bibles, Christians of convenience, freelance racists, misanthropic frat boys, shrieking midgets of AM radio, tax cheats, nihilists in golf pants, brownshirts in pinstripes, sweatshop tycoons...Republicans: The No. 1 reason the rest of the world thinks we're deaf, dumb, and dangerous."

—Garrison Keillor

A Glimpse into the Conservative Utopia

Conservatives are working hard to build a society that realizes their dreams for total domination over America's political and cultural landscape.

Whether they succeed or fail will depend on your commitment to derailing their plans. To illustrate what's at stake, here's a glimpse into America's possible future, should conservatives have their unfettered way with the country.

NEWSPAPER HEADLINES CONSERVATIVES WOULD LOVE TO SEE

★ Federal Government Axed as Part of Tea-Party Budget Deal, Merged into Subsidiary of Koch Industries

★ Ford Announces New F-150 to Run on Coal and Panda

★ Hippie Protesters Occupying Wall Street Declared Enemy Combatants, Rounded Up and Thrown in Gitmo

★ Obama Presidential Library to Break Ground in Kenya

★ Republicans Reform Social Security; Seniors Now Required to Fight for Benefits on Fox Reality Show Hosted by Steve Doocy

★ Congress Votes to Require L-Chip in TV Sets, Blocking All Liberal News Channels and Allowing for 100% Fact-Free Viewing

★ Education Secretary Palin Updates Textbooks to Include How Jesus Killed Dinosaurs for Trying to Take Guns from Cavemen

★ President Perry's National Prayer Rally Cures Homosexuality; *E!* Network to be Replaced by Fishing Channel

- ★ NASCAR's Kyle Busch named Secretary of Transportation
- ★ Majestic Toupee Causes Trump National Monument to Run Over Budget
- ★ Republicans Spare PBS; Grover Norquist Replaces Grover from *Sesame Street*
- ★ Congress Outsourced to India in Cost-Cutting Move; Interns Must Travel Overseas to be Sexually Harassed
- ★ Supreme Court Stops Ohio Recount, Names Exxon Mobil as U.S. President Over Challenger GE
- ★ GOP Lowers Tax Rate for Top 1% to 1%; Revenue Shortfall to Be Offset with Tax Hikes on Unemployed Seniors and Blood of Public School Students
- ★ Halliburton's New Soylent Green Product Single-Handedly Saving Economy; Poor and Unemployed are Practically Disappearing
- ★ Obama Impeached for Crimes against Capitalism

Don't think it could ever happen? Well, nobody thought the guy from *Kindergarten Cop* would be governor of the fifth largest economy in the world, but it happened…twice! Not to put too much pressure on you, but if you don't do your part to help frustrate their plans, the conservative utopians will have won.

★ **CHAPTER 3** ★

Can't We All Just Get Along?

"As Americans, we must ask ourselves: Are we really so different? Must we stereotype those who disagree with us? Do we truly believe that ALL red-state residents are ignorant, racist, fascist, knuckle-dragging, NASCAR-obsessed, cousin-marrying, roadkill-eating, tobacco juice-dribbling, gun-fondling, religious, fanatic rednecks; or that ALL blue-state residents are godless, unpatriotic, pierced-nose, Volvo-driving, France-loving, left-wing, communist, latte-sucking, tofu-chomping, holistic-wacko, neurotic, vegan, weenie perverts?"

—**Dave Barry**

Let's face it. Our great nation has been divided along fierce partisan lines ever since the days of our Founding Fathers, when even our finest powdered-wig-wearing, silk-stocking-strutting statesmen exchanged bitter recriminations over who was the bigger girlie-man.

With liberals and conservatives, Democrats and Republicans, and blue staters and red staters growing more polarized by the day, is there any hope left of finding common ground? The answer is yes. But before we get to that, let's first take stock of America's current state of disunion to discover exactly how deeply and ridiculously divided we have become.

A Day in the Life of Conservatives vs. Liberals

Conservatives and liberals may live in the same cities and breathe the same air, but they might as well be gliding along two separate planes of existence.

A Day in the Life of a Conservative	A Day in the Life of a Liberal
★ **7:00 a.m.**	
Wake up, flip on Fox News, find out what to be afraid of today	Wake up, turn on MSNBC, find out what to be outraged by today.
★ **8:00 a.m.**	
Bible study	Home Bikram yoga
★ **8:30 a.m.**	
Blare Rush Limbaugh while idling at McDonald's drive-through	Read *High Times* while sitting at a juice bar sipping wheat grass.
★ **9:00 a.m.**	
Arrive at work, secure rights to drill in ancient panda den	Arrive at work, begin sorting through frivolous lawsuits to prepare for filing
★ **10:00 a.m.**	
Update Facebook with pictures from this week's NRA spotted-owl BBQ	Update Facebook with pictures from shamanic drum circle

A Day in the Life of a Conservative	A Day in the Life of a Liberal
★ **11:00 a.m.**	
Log on to the *Drudge Report* to read about latest terrorist threat involving gay illegal immigrants posing as abortion doctors	Log on to the *Huffington Post* to read about Republican plans to build waterboarding theme park on National Mall
★ **12:00 p.m.**	
Eat half a deer burger (left over from weekend hunt), wash down with Bud, throw the rest away	Cleansing fast! No lunch today
★ **1:00 p.m.**	
Buy 100-share lot of Halliburton stock in anticipation of war with Iran	Buy solar-powered laptop case to offset guilt for racing against a Prius in your new Nissan Leaf for zero-emissions supremacy

A Day in the Life of a Conservative	A Day in the Life of a Liberal
★ 2:00 p.m.	
Walk around the office, remind everyone who the "job creator" is	Walk around the office, try to get coworkers to sign petition to change this year's office Christmas party to a nondenominational winter solstice celebration
★ 3:00 p.m.	
Gas up Hummer, reposition Confederate flag on window, clean homeless person off grille	Pump air in bicycle tires, lecture passing drivers about evils of internal combustion engine
★ 4:00 p.m.	
Stop by drugstore for Vicodin prescription, report suspicious-looking cashier to INS for deportation	Stop by holistic healing center to see if the South American pygmy healing root has arrived in hopes of curing venereal diseases picked up at Burning Man

A Day in the Life of a Conservative	A Day in the Life of a Liberal
★ **5:00 p.m.**	
Stop by Walmart, buy booze and ammo	Stop by Whole Foods, spend $60 for a free-range beet salad and a mineral water from France
★ **6:00 p.m.**	
Join the guys at Hooters to watch ESPN and ogle the waitstaff over a couple of pitchers	Join fellow tree huggers to block commuter traffic until the city agrees to build a "toad tunnel" allowing frogs to safely cross busy street
★ **7:00 p.m.**	
Sit down to family dinner and enjoy a delicious Godfather's pizza in honor of future president Herman Cain	Occupy your local country club, eat the rich, then recycle their monocles and top hats in a wealthy compost heap
★ **8:00 p.m.**	
Watch *The O'Reilly Factor* for fair and balanced news	Watch *The Daily Show* for fair and balanced news

A Day in the Life of a Conservative	A Day in the Life of a Liberal
★ **8:30 p.m.**	
Put the kids to bed after reading them *Help Mom! There Are Liberals Under My Bed!*	Put the kids to bed after reading them *Mommy, Mama, and Me*
★ **9:00 p.m.**	
Log on to Hot Air to read new and inventive ways to continue to blame Obama	Log on to Media Matters to read new and inventive ways to continue to blame Bush
★ **10:00 p.m.**	
Have missionary sex with spouse (if on a business trip, have illicit tryst in hotel bathroom with intern)	Invite the neighbors over for Tantric group orgy while listening to Tuvan throat singing
★ **11:00 p.m.**	
Recite prayers, await the Rapture	Smoke joint, fall asleep

"The Democrats are the party of government activism, the party that says government can make you richer, smarter, taller, and get the chickweed out of your lawn. Republicans are the party that says government doesn't work, and then get elected and prove it."

—P. J. O'Rourke

Battle of the Bumper Stickers

There's no better illustration of the stark partisan split  than the ideological battle that conservatives and liberals are waging every day on America's roadways.

POPULAR LIBERAL BUMPER STICKERS

★ Tea Parties Are For Little Girls With Imaginary Friends

★ The Republican Party: Our Bridge To The 11th Century

★ My President Killed Osama Bin Laden. How About Yours?

★ Fine…I Evolved, You Didn't

★ Don't Like Socialism? Get Off The Highway

* Insurance Companies Are Republican Death Panels
* May The Fetus You Save Be Gay
* GOP Family Values—Your Rights Begin At Conception And End At Birth
* If You Cut Off My Reproductive Rights, Can I Cut Off Yours?
* I'd Vote For A Republican, But I'm Allergic To Nuts
* That Stuff Trickling Down On You Isn't Money
* Due To Recent Budget Cuts, The Light At The End Of The Tunnel Has Been Turned Off
* Killing For Peace Is Like Screwing For Virginity
* When You're Old And Eating Cat Food, You Can Thank A Republican
* Voting Is Like Driving A Car. Choose (R) To Move Backward. Choose (D) To Move Forward.
* Fox News: Rich People Paying Rich People To Tell Middle Class People To Blame Poor People

POPULAR CONSERVATIVE BUMPER STICKERS

* Don't Blame Me! I Voted For The American
* Occupy A Job!
* I'll Keep My Freedom, My Guns, And My Money. You Can Keep The Change!

- ★ Does This Ass Make My Car Look Fat? (With A Picture Of Obama)
- ★ Global Warming: The #1 Threat To Unicorns
- ★ I'd Rather Be Waterboarding
- ★ I'd Rather Be A Conservative Nut Job Than A Liberal With No Nuts And No Job!
- ★ Environmentalism: Just Another Religious Doomsday Cult
- ★ Work Harder! Millions On Welfare Depend On You!
- ★ In Case Of Rapture, This Car Will Be Unmanned
- ★ If You're Gonna Burn Our Flag, Wrap Yourself In It First
- ★ I Only Burn Fuel Because Burning Hippies Is Illegal
- ★ Somewhere In Kenya, A Village Is Missing Its Idiot
- ★ Silly Liberal, Paychecks Are For Workers
- ★ If Ignorance Is Bliss, You Must Be One Happy Liberal

"Conservative, n: a statesman who is enamored of existing evils, as distinguished from the Liberal, who wishes to replace them with others."

—Ambrose Bierce

What Liberals Say vs. What Conservatives Hear

Most liberals and conservatives who have spent any time in the partisan trenches quickly discover that even basic attempts at communication can be utterly futile. Thanks to ingrained stereotypes, built-in defense mechanisms, and intense partisan conditioning, a liberal may say one thing, but a conservative is almost certain to hear something else. As you can see here, it's not pretty:

What liberals say: We must raise taxes on the top 1% and spread the wealth around.

What conservatives hear: I'm not going to work. Give me money. Take care of my lazy ass.

What liberals say: We must occupy Wall Street and bring down those greedy bastards.

What conservatives hear: I don't shower.

What liberals say: Corporations are NOT people!

What conservatives hear: I hate free markets and would rather live in China!

What liberals say: I'm tired of listening to religious

nut cases and puritanical prudes trying to dictate what I do in the bedroom or what I can do with my body.

What conservatives hear: Let's go have sex with a horse and then worship Satan.

What liberals say: The media does not have a liberal bias.
What conservatives hear: Baaaaaaaa. I'm a sheep.

What liberals say: Make love, not war.
What conservatives hear: I heart terrorists!

What liberals say: Republicans hate all poor people, minorities, and the elderly.
What conservatives hear: Hey, it's Kanye West!

What liberals say: Bush wrecked the economy. Everything is Bush's fault!
What conservatives hear: Our plan to fix the economy crapped out so all we got left is "blame the last guy."

What liberals say: Conservatives are all a bunch of uneducated, healthcare-denying, waterboard-loving, doomsday-preaching, corporate-crime-forgiving, NRA-worshipping, knuckle-dragging, Bible-banging bigots who have done more to destroy American democracy than Al Qaeda ever dreamed.

What conservatives hear: I hate America, I hate freedom, I hate puppies, and welcome to the *Rachel Maddow Show.*

What Conservatives Say vs. What Liberals Hear

There's no better luck on the flip side:

What conservatives say: Obama is a Muslim Kenyan socialist Nazi and probably the Antichrist.
What liberals hear: I was homeschooled by Fox News.

What conservatives say: If we cut taxes on the rich and cut spending, it will create millions of jobs, reduce the deficit, and make the economy boom.
What liberals hear: Unicorns for everybody!

What conservatives say: Democrats are communist fascist Nazi socialists.
What liberals hear: I have no idea what any of those words actually mean, I just have no ideas of my own.

What conservatives say: Obamacare is unconstitutional!

What liberals hear: Three cheers for letting the uninsured die!

What conservatives say: We need to crack down on illegal immigration.

What liberals hear: I'm racist and afraid of brown people. Better grill them on an electrified fence before they knock up my daughter.

What conservatives say: We need to defend the institution of marriage and stop the gay agenda.

What liberals hear: I'm a closeted homosexual who likes to frequent airport men's rooms.

What conservatives say: Democrats are coming after your money, your guns, and your God.

What liberals hear: Hey, here's some irrational fear to trick really stupid people into feeling good about voting against their own interests.

What conservatives say: Democrats want to bring your grandmother before a death panel.

What liberals hear: I'm watching Glenn Beck TV and I'm off my meds.

What conservatives say: We need to dismantle the job-killing EPA.

What liberals hear: Hey kids, free arsenic and mercury for everyone!

What conservatives say: We need to reduce our dependency on foreign oil by pursuing oil exploration at home.

What liberals hear: I hate national parks and coastlines! Let's improve them by adding giant oil rigs and pollution. Besides how cute are pelicans when they're covered in oil?

What conservatives say: This is a Christian nation, and our laws should reflect that.

What liberals hear: I'm sick of Jewish people taking more holidays than me.

What conservatives say: Liberals are all a bunch of Hollywood-loving, gun-grabbing, stem-cell-sucking, abortion-promoting, tax-hiking, troop-slandering, gay-marrying socialists who are hell-bent on destroying America.

What liberals hear: Good evening, and welcome to *The Sean Hannity Show.*

> *"What side shall prevail in this epic electoral tilt? Who shall control the future of Fortress America? Will we be, as the Republicans desire, a nation of wealthy, heavily armed white men, befouling the air and water in a ceaseless quest for profits, beholden to no laws but those of our Lord and Savior Jesus Christ? Or shall we instead embrace the Democrats' vision of a namby-pamby, quasi-socialist republic with an all-homosexual army flamboyantly defending a citizenry suckling at the foul teat of government welfare? The choice is yours, fair maiden America, for the name of this feudal system is Democracy."*
>
> —Stephen Colbert

Common Enemies We Can All Agree to Hate

OK, now that it's abundantly clear how hopelessly estranged and deranged the two warring sides have become, it's time to find that elusive common ground.

It's been said that what divides us as a country is not nearly as strong as what unites us. And what could unite us more than our common enemies? With that in mind, let us embark on the path to bipartisan unity by taking a moment to jointly revile some of the most odious miscreants and evildoers that liberals and conservatives can agree to hate.

You can, of course, never go wrong bashing the likes of Al Qaeda, Mahmoud Ahmadinejad, corporate criminals, pedophiles, and people who talk on their cell phones during movies. But if you really want to bond with conservatives, try trash-talking the following enemies of freedom, all of whom pose a more immediate threat to our collective sanity.

THE MEDIA

It's a sad commentary on the state of the news media when Americans identify comedian Jon Stewart as the most trusted newsman on television. Whether you think the mainstream media is guilty of liberal or conservative bias, it can usually be counted on to botch the facts and distort the truth in the race to get the story wrong first. Sure, there are some intrepid journalists doing important work, but then there's Piers Morgan. As a whole, the establishment media is a brainless, sensationalistic, and unstoppable force that you can rely on to saturate the airwaves with wall-to-wall coverage of the latest missing blond girl, ignore the current genocidal war in

Africa, blindly regurgitate partisan talking points, and, occasionally, make up stories out of whole cloth. The best you can hope for these days are partially correct weather and traffic reports.

> *The press can hold its magnifying glass up to our problems and illuminate problems heretofore unseen, or it can use its magnifying glass to light ants on fire, and then perhaps host a week of shows on the sudden, unexpected dangerous-flaming-ant epidemic. If we amplify everything, we hear nothing.*
>
> —Jon Stewart at the Rally
> to Restore Sanity and/or Fear

TSA AGENTS

It's not their fault that their job sucks, it's the evil pleasure they derive from patting down an eighty-seven-year-old grandma who might be concealing a four-ounce tube of hemorrhoid medicine in her denture case. Or, in one actual case, going through a woman's luggage, finding a sex toy, and leaving a handwritten note that said, "GET YOUR FREAK ON GIRL."

The TSA's motto is "Your safety is our priority," but a popular Internet meme suggested some fitting alternatives: "We are now free to move about your pants," "We handle more packages than USPS," "It's not a grope. It's a freedom pat," and "If we did our job any better we'd have to buy you dinner first."

PORK-BARREL SPENDERS

You and your conservative pals should be able to agree that the following actual uses of taxpayer money (approved by Democrats and Republicans alike) should be considered criminal: $143 million to protect the Giant Lava Lamp in Soap Lake, Washington, against terrorist attack; $10 million to protect a toilet seat art museum in Alamo Heights, Texas, against terrorist attack; $7 million spent by the Army each year to sponsor NASCAR Sprint Cup driver Ryan Newman; nearly $600,000 to study why chimps throw feces; over $175,000 to study how cocaine enhances the sex drive of Japanese quail; over $6,000 to purchase snow cone ice-making machines for emergencies in Michigan; and $800,000 in "stimulus funds" spent to study the impact of a "genital-washing program" on men in South Africa. This is particularly wasteful because surely there are men in America who would gladly wash their genitals for half that amount.

OFFSHORERS

When it comes to big business and tax policy, Republicans and Democrats agree on virtually nothing. But one area where both sides should be able to find common ground is in vilifying those soulless bastards who exploit huge corporate tax breaks, only to move all the jobs offshore. How about we pass a constitutional amendment so the next time they need a bailout, they automatically get re-routed to a call center in India where a guy named "Bob" will happily waste three hours of their time before arbitrarily disconnecting them.

WESTBORO BAPTIST CHURCH

Another hate group masquerading as a church, this loathsome assemblage of mouth-breathing Neanderthals has made a name for itself by desecrating the American flag and picketing the funerals of soldiers and famous people with their gay-bashing placards. Even the KKK got involved in protesting these jackasses. Yes, this is something even you and your local Grand Dragon or Imperial Wizard can agree on. The Westboro Baptist Church freaks are such heartless and vile souls that no right-thinking Republican, Democrat, or reputable institution could ever possibly defend them—with the notable exception of the U.S. Supreme Court, which upheld their right to terrorize people at funerals. Stupid First Amendment.

OWNERS AND PLAYERS WHO GIVE US STRIKES AND LOCKOUTS

One place Republicans, Democrats, and independents should be able to find common ground is in their hatred of greedy billionaires and spoiled millionaires who take away our sports when they can't work out their differences. Players, you are grown men who get paid obscene amounts of money to play with a ball. Owners, you are already billionaires, not to mention all the chicks you get just for saying, "By the way, I own the Dallas Mavericks." No one feels sorry for either of you, so figure it out. It is with one clear voice we say, "Suck it up, professional sports." No American wins when Lakers vs. Celtics is replaced by *A Very Kardashian Christmas*.

REALITY SHOW STARS

Is there any bigger waste of time than reality television? OK, maybe listening to people talk about reality television. With all the problems in this country, why do we have to hear about these people every day? Who cares which washed-up celebrity is a better dancer? Did we really need to see Tom DeLay's gyrating ass on television (an image so horrifying, no amount of bleach could remove it from our eyes)? Do those "real housewives" look like anyone you've ever met in real life? You're having a fight in a kitchen about some soup—for the love of God, why? And seriously, enough shows about freakishly large families. Isn't flying terrifying enough without the prospect of getting stuck on a twelve-hour flight behind *Kate Plus Eight*? Please bring back the one reality show we could all agree on, *COPS*!

"I view America like this: 70 to 80 percent [are] pretty reasonable people that truthfully, if they sat down, even on contentious issues, would get along. And the other 20 percent of the country run it."

—Jon Stewart

★ **CHAPTER 4** ★

Basic Training

"Irreverence is the champion of liberty and its only sure defense."

—Mark Twain

There's a right way to engage conservatives in combat and a wrong way. The right way will enable you to make forceful arguments, win hearts and minds, and be greeted as a liberator. The wrong way will alienate your opponents, make them harden their position, and get you kicked out of public places.

Unfortunately, due to inadequate preparation and training—or sheer self-delusion—many people embark on the wrong path. To help you gird for battle and avert certain disaster, we'll show you in this chapter how to avoid key pitfalls, pick the right fights, hone your bullshit detector, and turn arguments to your advantage by following some basic rules of engagement.

> *"The definition of insanity is doing the same thing over and over again and expecting different results."*
>
> **—Albert Einstein, attributed**

The Seven Habits of Highly Ineffective Partisans

As with many things in life, we are often our own worst enemies. These seven habits are like kryptonite to the partisan warrior and must be painstakingly avoided.

1. PEDDLING CONSPIRACY THEORIES

Right-wingers have been ridiculed for popping out paranoid conspiratorial nonsense like Pez ever since Obama took office. But they don't have a monopoly on this particular kind of crazy. Liberals have been known to dabble in the dark arts of conspiracy peddling too—claiming that 9/11 was an inside job, Sarah Palin isn't actually Trig's mom, and that Dick Cheney is an evil

Sith Lord (OK, the last one may actually be true). Even if you feel you have rock-solid intelligence from the Nigerian prince who emailed you directly, don't go there. You just end up looking like an idiot. There are plenty of good arguments to make without bringing in the vast conspiracy of little green men on the grassy knoll. And besides, as anyone who has worked in government will tell you, the government isn't competent enough to pull off a decent conspiracy.

2. LETTING CONSERVATIVES MAKE YOU CRAZY

Conservatives will undoubtedly drive you nutty with their brick-like imperviousness to basic facts and reason. But remember, that's their goal. They want to see the veins pop out of your forehead and cartoon steam emit from your ears. Don't let them succeed. No matter what they say, keep a cool head. If you end up having a Charlie Sheen-style meltdown and find yourself blurting out that you have "tiger blood" and "fire-breathing fists," while insisting, "I'm not bipolar, I'm bi-winning, I win here and I win there," you're definitely not winning.

3. LUMPING UNRELATED ISSUES TOGETHER

Nothing screams political sophistication like a protest to save the whales, shut down Wall Street, legalize gay marriage, protect unions, stop the sale of genetically modified yams, and impeach Fox News. Pick one issue or cause at a time and, for the love of logic, stay on message.

4. USING NAZI ANALOGIES

George W. Bush wasn't Hitler. Obama isn't Hitler. The next Republican president liberals will be tempted to call Hitler won't be Hitler either. Hitler was Hitler. Enough already, because do you know who else liked over-the-top political analogies? Hitler.

5. PICKING FIGHTS WITH OTHER LIBERALS

There's no denying that some liberals are utterly clueless and need a good smack in the head, but why do conservatives' dirty work for them? Nothing is more self-defeating than expending valuable energy tussling with another liberal while you both lose sight of the bigger picture. (Just look at what all those Naderites did in 2000, screwing over the liberal cause and giving us eight years of Bush.) Any time you engage in partisan fratricide instead of focusing on the battles that really matter, picture Mr. Burns from *The Simpsons* tenting his evil fingers and saying, "*Excellent.*" If you help your enemy divide and conquer, you end up doing more damage than conservatives could hope to do in their darkest, tea-drenched dreams.

6. RESORTING TO NAME-CALLING AT THE OUTSET

It's generally not good strategy to begin an argument by calling your opponent a heartless, tobacco-juice-dribbling moron or a witless, book-burning buffoon. Ad hominem attacks are a sign of weakness—a tactic that ineffective partisans resort to when they're too lazy or ill-informed to make real arguments. Instead, save your insults for detonation after you've *lost* an argument, when all else has failed (see After-*words:* 125,000 Ways to Insult Conservatives). For example, if you've just tried to argue that Obama will bring about world peace and your opponent points out that he has launched more cruise missiles than any Nobel Peace Prize winner in history, that's a good time to hit the eject button and deploy your parachute as you say, "Well, at least he's not a gap-toothed, Armageddon-yearning hypochristian like you."

7. ARGUING WITH IDIOTS

"Do not argue with an idiot," Mark Twain once said. "He will drag you down to his level and beat you with experience." Better to save the oxygen for those capable of rational discourse (even if this makes attending NAS-CAR races less fun). If you must argue with an idiot, different rules apply. Take humorist Dave Barry's advice: (1) drink liquor; (2) make things up; (3) use meaningless but weighty-sounding words and phrases ("vis-à-vis," "per se," "ipso facto," "ergo"); (4) use snappy and irrelevant comebacks ("You're begging the question," "You're being defensive," "You're so linear"); and (5) go ahead and compare your opponent to Hitler.

> *"I argue very well. Ask any of my remaining friends. I can win an argument on any topic, against any opponent. People know this and steer clear of me at parties. Often as a sign of their great respect, they don't even invite me."*
> —Dave Barry

Do You Suffer from Argumentile Dysfunction?

Now let's identify whether you're predisposed to any of the seven deadly habits. Answer these questions about how you would handle yourself in the following situations.

1. You're at a family gathering, discussing the economy, when your uncle Max starts crying poverty about how he's being taxed to death by that fascist communist Obama, who keeps flushing money down the toilet and running up the deficit. Which of the following would you do?

_____A. Tell him he's a moron who doesn't know what he's talking about, since a fascist communist is like a Christian Muslim or a vegan carnivore.

_____B. Offer to get him some tea, bring it to him, dump it in his lap, and scald him while screaming, "It's a Tea Party!"

_____C. Quote Karl Marx, Noam Chomsky, and Michael Moore until his head is about to explode. As he attempts to leave in a huff, grab his wallet and spread his wealth around the table.

_____D. Remind him that he's an unemployed former public worker who's living off a fat disability check and all the cheap Vicodin he can get courtesy of the Bush prescription drug program.

_____E. Let him know that the biggest sources of our deficit—two wars, massive tax breaks for the rich, and an unpaid-for Medicare prescription drug benefit—were all inherited by Obama from Bush, who was to fiscal responsibility what Glenn Beck is to sanity.

2. You're hanging out in your college dorm, passing around a bong, when one of your friends confesses that he's decided to vote for a Republican in the next election. Which of the following would you do?

_____A. Gather up every liberal you know and have an immediate intervention. That's right, a road trip to the Bonnaroo Music Festival!

_____B. Tell every girl he tries to hook up with that he's planning on voting Republican. Nothing says "cock block" like GOP.

_____C. Fail to realize what was said until *after* the election because you were too high.

_____D. Tell him that a conservative is a liberal who's been mugged and a liberal is a conservative who's been arrested. Then have him arrested for drug possession.

_____E. Tell him you never realized he made over $250,000 a year, since there's no other earthly reason to vote Republican. And since that must be the case, tell him it's time to fork over the $200 he owes you after he and his Republican friends crashed your party, drank all your booze, ordered a dozen pizzas, gave them away to a bunch of frat boys, and stuck you with the bill.

3. You are visiting a friend in Arizona when you witness a couple of Hispanic males being questioned by the cops. Your friend says, "Hope they send them back to Mexico." Which of the following would you do?

_____A. Yell at your friend for being racist because those men are clearly from Nicaragua.

_____B. Tell him that Arizona is exactly like another place where you had to show your papers: Nazi Germany.

_____C. Explain how it would be better if Arizona built a wall around itself to keep the immigrants from getting in and the idiots from getting out.

_____D. Grab a can of spray tan, apply it to his face, kick him out of the car, and wish him well trying to find his way back to Los Angeles via Mexico.

_____E. Call him on the fact that most Americans don't work half as hard as illegal immigrants do, while getting paid practically no money. Point out how he would never survive working in a field for sixteen hours a day when he can barely handle surfing porn at his desk for six hours with a two-hour lunch thrown in.

If you answered E to the above questions, you're ready to move on to the next section. If not, this may help explain why you haven't been winning many arguments lately (and possibly why you don't get invited to social functions anymore).

"A diplomat...is a person who can tell you to go to hell in such a way that you actually look forward to the trip."

—**Caskie Stinnett**

How Not to Be an Asshole

Tempted as you may be to blurt out obscenities, hurl insults, or pepper-spray your opponent, successful arguing strategy (and the laws of polite society) require that you employ more civilized tactics (at least at the beginning of an argument).

This chart will show you how to channel your fury in a way that—while admittedly less satisfying than, say, telling your opponent to go perform an anatomically impossible sex act—will help encourage better diplomatic relations.

What You'll Be Tempted to Say	How to Translate that into Diplo-Speak
"Are you completely freaking insane?"	"I'm not sure I'm following the reasoning behind your argument."
"Did your lobotomy leave a scar?"	"Do you honestly believe that?"
"Which dark crevice of your ass did you pull that from?"	"How do you back up that claim?"
"Stupid inbred redneck."	"I can't identify with what you're saying."
"What do the demons say when they come for you at night?"	"How did you arrive at that conclusion?"

What You'll Be Tempted to Say	How to Translate that into Diplo-Speak
"Does your cable company only carry the Fox Network?"	"Let me suggest some news sources that report actual facts."
"Do I need to speak slower, with fewer syllables?"	"I'm not sure we're communicating."
"Hey, you mouth-breathing teabagger, the Dark Ages called—they want their ideology back."	"I think you have some ideas that may be a little regressive."
"Isn't it great that we live in a country where even a total douche bag like yourself is free to utter whatever mindless drivel pops into his head?"	"You have a right to your opinion."

What You'll Be Tempted to Say	How to Translate that into Diplo-Speak
"I'd rather undergo waterboarding torture at the hands of Dick Cheney himself than listen to another word you have to say."	"I think we're going to have to agree to disagree."
"If I had $100 for every time you said something true, I'd be poor as shit."	"Better recheck your facts, Boehner."
"Your parents were clearly brother and sister."	"You obviously come from a very close family."
"Did you eat a lot of paint chips when you were a kid?"	"You must have had a very challenging childhood."

What You'll Be Tempted to Say	How to Translate that into Diplo-Speak
"Listen, you brain-dead, naturally unselected moron, you'd be out of your depth in a parking lot puddle."	"I'm not sure this is really a fair fight."
"How is it even possible for a sentient being to arrive at that kind of breathtakingly idiotic conclusion?"	"If I agreed with you, we'd both be wrong."
"Sorry, Mrs. Bachmann, but that voice in your head is not God. Take your meds."	"Have you considered seeking professional help?"
"What planet do you fucking live on?"	"I think we have radically different notions of what constitutes reality."

"If you've got them by the balls, their hearts and minds will follow."

—**Anonymous**

The Ten Commandments of Partisan Warfare

Here is your guide to becoming a model partisan.

1. USE HUMOR AS A WEAPON

Making humorous observations—and demonstrating an ability to laugh at yourself—can be an effective tool to help disarm your opponents. They'll be much more likely to listen to the next thing you have to say. Once you've cracked a joke or two and lulled them into a sense of complacency, that's when you move in for the kill. If funny isn't your thing, quote professional quipsters like Jon Stewart or unintentional comedians like Sarah Palin, and bear in mind what Will Rogers once said: "There's no trick to being a humorist when you have the whole government working for you."

Example: "If 'con' is the opposite of pro, then isn't Congress the opposite of progress? Or did we just fucking blow your mind?!?" —Jon Stewart, *America (The Book): A Citizen's Guide to Democracy Inaction*

2. KEEP IT SIMPLE

Making a long-winded, complex, nuanced argument to a conservative will get you nowhere because (a) conservatives don't do complexity or nuance; and (b) their Fox News diet restricts them from digesting information that isn't delivered in crisp, sugary spoonfuls. That's why you need to have some pithy sound bites at your disposal to use as openers or rejoinders. We're not suggesting that you dumb down your arguments. But you should try to distill your basic message to a slogan you could fit on a cardboard sign. (If it doesn't work, then you'll have a handy piece of cardboard you can use to beat them over the head.)

Examples: "If only the war on poverty were a real war, then we would actually be putting money into it"; "Obama is not a brown-skinned, anti-war socialist who gives away free health care. You're thinking of Jesus"; "Against gay marriage? Then don't have one."

3. FRAME THE DEBATE TO YOUR ADVANTAGE

Always stay on the offensive and make your case by presenting each issue according to your beliefs and values, *not theirs.* If you let your adversary define the terms and frame the discussion, they win.

Example: Look at what Bill Maher does here to

flip around a common conservative talking point: "If conservatives get to call universal health care 'socialized medicine,' I get to call private, for-profit health care 'soulless, vampire bastards making money off human pain.'" Any time you can shift a discussion to more comfortable territory with a clever quip or humorous observation, you set yourself up to win.

4. DAZZLE THEM WITH METAPHORS

You can pack your arguments with extra punch through strategic use of metaphors and analogies. Not only will they help to illustrate your points more vividly, but if you can employ a little humor, you might even coax a chuckle out of your opponents to help lower their defenses.

Examples: When a conservative makes a ridiculous claim, such as crediting George W. Bush for killing Osama bin Laden, don't just say it's ridiculous. Illustrate it with an analogy: "It's like when you open a pickle jar and somebody says, 'Yeah, but I loosened it,'" joked Jimmy Kimmel. "It's like Edward John Smith, the captain of the Titanic, taking credit for the results of the 1998 Academy Awards," wrote Andrew Cohen in *The Atlantic*. "It's like King George III taking credit for the United States of America after England lost the colonies," noted the *Huffington Post*'s Ross Luippold.

5. RIDICULE THE OPPOSITION

As the famed left-wing rabble-rouser Saul Alinsky advises in his classic tome, *Rules for Radicals*, "Ridicule is man's most potent weapon. It's hard to counterattack ridicule, and it infuriates the opposition, which then reacts to your advantage." This may explain why right-wingers are always so infuriated—they're so easy to ridicule!

Example: "Donald Trump has been saying that he's going to run for president as a Republican—which is surprising, since I just assumed he was running as a joke. Donald Trump often appears on Fox, which is ironic, because a fox often appears on Donald Trump's head." —*Saturday Night Live*'s Seth Meyers, speaking at the 2011 White House Correspondents' Dinner, where Donald Trump sat stone-faced in the audience. Unable to take a joke, Trump looked like an even bigger idiot afterward when he griped that the dinner was "inappropriate" and called Meyers "a stutterer."

6. HIGHLIGHT HYPOCRISY

Nothing undermines an argument faster than exposing hypocritical behavior, contradictory statements, and wholesale fakery—either on the part of your opponents or on the part of the politicians they're defending.

There are few sights as satisfying as watching exposed hypocrites grasp at fig leaves to cover their shame. Unless, of course, that hypocrite is a family-values Republican congressman who has been caught with his pants down while filming an abstinence video with his mistress, in which case, you might want to avert your eyes (true story—ex-Rep. Mark Souder (R-IN)).

Example: "Newt Gingrich is so pro-marriage, he can't stop doing it. He is so morally upright, that he's only had sex after he was married. Just not always to the woman he was married to." —Stephen Colbert

7. USE CONSERVATIVES' OWN WORDS AGAINST THEM

One of the best ways to make a convincing argument to a conservative is to let another conservative do it for you. Any time you can quote a conservative to support your point, it's a twofer: you cite an authority who, in their minds, is unimpeachable, and you make their heads hurt as they struggle with the cognitive dissonance.

Examples: When they say "Screw all the unions," point out that it was the great socialist Ronald Reagan who once said, "Where free unions and collective bargaining are forbidden, freedom is lost." Or when they say it's fiscal insanity to keep raising the debt ceiling, point out that George W. Bush did it seven times and Reagan did it eighteen times, without any Republican protest, with Reagan warning that default would lead to "denigration of the full faith and credit of the United States" and create "incalculable damage." Tell them it's a shame that conservatives have moved so far to the right that Reagan would be pushed out of the party today as a lily-livered leftist. (You can find more damning quotes from conservatives in Chapter 8.)

8. MAKE YOUR OPPONENTS DEFEAT THEMSELVES

One of the most effective arguing techniques, utilized by lawyers and others skilled in the art of persuasion, simply involves posing a series of leading questions. It's known as the Socratic method, and it's easy to employ. All you need to do is ask questions that will box in your opponent and expose the gaping holes in their thinking. Demonstrating that someone is wrong is always more effective than telling someone they're wrong.

Example: Try a line of questioning like this: "Do you think all Americans should pay their fair share in taxes? Do you think it's fair if someone making over $1 billion a year pays a tax rate of 17 percent, while you and I are paying, on average, about 25 percent? How about we ask that billionaire to pay the same tax rate as the guy he pays to wash his private jet with the tears of Tea Partiers he pays to cry about his taxes being so high?"

9. PREY ON THEIR FEARS

Researchers who looked at the brains of liberals and conservatives made an interesting discovery: conservatives have a larger area of the brain that processes fear and identifies threats, while liberals have more brain space dedicated to processing complex information. That means if you want to get conservatives to listen to you, you need to use your considerable brain power to come up with inventive ways to scare the crap out of them.

Examples: Tell your opponent you have received privileged information from Michael Moore that a cabal of Marxists in the White House is plotting with FEMA to release flying monkeys that will open up a drive-through abortion clinic in his church. If that doesn't get a rise, tell him that bearded ACLU communists are conspiring with underwear bombers to take him hostage and force him to gay-marry an illegal immigrant in a mosque at Ground Zero. It doesn't really matter what you say, just try to get them panicking. Suddenly their worries about a government takeover of health care will pale by comparison.

10. LAUNCH A SNEAK ATTACK

If conservatives think they are talking to a hopeless liberal, you may never get a chance to win them over because they'll shun you as they would a vegan at a pig pickin'. That's why in some instances, it can be strategically useful to pretend to be a moderate or a liberal who is open to persuasion. The goal is to rope them in, thinking they may be able to convert you, and then unleash a Trojan horse-style sneak attack when they're least expecting it.

Example: Start by bad mouthing a liberal (say, Al Sharpton or Sean Penn) to build street cred. Take it up a notch by grumbling about how Sharia law is taking hold at the post office. Mention you've decided to vote against the Democratic candidate in the next election. Suddenly you will find yourself welcomed into the conservative inner sanctum, invited to pro-life bake sales, offered discounts on guns, and given Kool-Aid (don't drink it!). There are lots of things you can do once you're on the inside: become a mole or parcel out extremely bad advice. Or if all goes well, you can angle your way into becoming a featured speaker at a Tea Party convention. Once the cameras are rolling, use the opportunity to denounce the idiocy of Tea Partiers from the podium—quickly, before security wrestles you to the ground. Get the footage on YouTube immediately. Gripe loudly about the intolerance of Tea Partiers while making the rounds on the talk show circuit, and then secure a book deal. Battle won.

> *"When you ask me that question, I'm going to revert to my ethnic heritage and ask you a question. On what planet do you spend most of your time? You stand there with a picture of the president defaced to look like Hitler and compare the effort to increase health care to the Nazis...Trying to have a conversation with you would be like trying to argue with a dining room table. I have no interest in doing it."*
>
> —Rep. Barney Frank (D-MA), dropping the smackdown on a Tea Partier at a town hall meeting

How to Avoid Unhinged Lunatics

There's nothing wrong with occasionally mixing it up with conservatives who have extreme views. It's the ones who have extreme personality disorders you should be concerned about. You know, those totally incapable of having an intelligent, thoughtful discussion about anything. They bicker instead of argue, rant instead of talk, and parrot instead of think.

These kinds of sociopaths can be found anywhere—ambushing perfect strangers at cocktail parties, holding entire families hostage at holiday time, and scarring their Facebook pages with rambling, Sarah Palin-style diatribes.

There is no use wasting perfectly good oxygen arguing with these people. You'll be much better off—and cut down on your Xanax bills—if you focus your energies on reasonable people capable of passing a field sanity test. Here's how to administer it:

★ Do they preface more than half their sentences with "Well, Glenn Beck says…"?

★ In place of the usual expletives, do they use "Olbermann," "Soros," "Pelosi," "Reid," or "Frisco"?

★ Do they frequently interrupt you mid-sentence with Joe Wilson-style heckles, such as "You lie!"?

★ Do they become instantly irate at the slightest of triggers? For example, if you say the word "Obama," do their faces turn visibly red and do their neck veins begin pulsating?

★ Have they handcuffed themselves to their guns,

just in case someone tries to pry them from their cold, dead hands?

★ Do they wear their stupidity on their person? For example, are they sporting a "Keep your government hands off my Medicare" button, still wearing a "McCain in the membrane" T-shirt from the 2008 election, or dangling teabags from body parts that shouldn't be exposed?

★ Do they refer to pepper spraying as "watering hippies"?

★ When you talk about tax cuts, do they become sexually aroused?

★ Do they have the same stock answer to everything? For example, do they frequently explain that liberals simply hate America, freedom, the flag, the troops, God, and kittens?

★ Are they prone to Tourette's-like outbursts in which they spasmodically denounce you as a "godless, terrorist-loving hippie," "stupid, baby-killing feminazi," or "coastal-dwelling pervert"?

★ At any point do they mention that if gay marriage becomes legal, it's only a matter of time before a couple is pronounced man and aardvark?

★ Have they already staked a Bristol Palin 2028 sign into their lawn?

★ Do they post holier-than-thou comments containing numerous Biblical quotes in online forums, and then urge you to "spread the word of God with love, asshole"?

★ Do they host a show on Fox called *The O'Reilly Factor*?

If the conservative in question exhibits any of the above behavior patterns, he or she has failed the field sanity test. Do yourself a favor—back away slowly and avoid these people as you would Charlie Sheen at a cocaine and hooker convention. Nothing good will ever come of talking to them.

Anyone else is fair game.

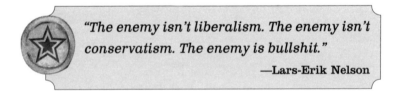

"The enemy isn't liberalism. The enemy isn't conservatism. The enemy is bullshit."

—**Lars-Erik Nelson**

How to Detect Bullshit

Let's state the obvious. Conservatives love to bullshit. We're not just talking about the professionals who promise us "fair and balanced" news or sell us bogus wars. Your average conservative on the street is skilled at slinging it, too.

To combat bullshit, it's important to first define what it is and what makes it so insidious.

"Bullshit is a greater enemy of the truth than lies are," says Harry Frankfurt, who literally wrote the book *On Bullshit*. Bullshitters, Frankfurt says, are distinguished by the fact that they couldn't care less about whether what they are saying is true. They have a completely different agenda. Bullshitters are mainly concerned with trying to wow, distract, or manipulate their audience, and they'll simply cherry-pick facts or make up things to fit their needs.

That's why bullshitters are such menaces to society. Their total lack of regard for the truth gives them free rein to manipulate people willy-nilly, so long as no one calls them on it. They also have one thing in common: they're trying to conceal something.

To help you calibrate your bullshit detector, here's a guide to the various bullshitting life forms that you are likely to encounter and what they are trying to hide.

THE FACT FABRICATORS
What they do: They present you with the "straight facts," which are actually faux facts, likely picked up from Fox

(or make that Faux) News. They'll make up anything to support their crumbling arguments, mismatch disjointed pieces of information to form a fact-esque facade, and reject any inconvenient facts as biased and likely socialist. When cornered by incontrovertible facts (e.g., gravity), they'll simply throw up a smoke screen and declare the facts to be open to debate.

What they're hiding: The fact that they have no interest in facts at all, and that they believe, as Ronald Reagan said, that "facts are stupid things."

THE KNOWLEDGE SUPREMACISTS

What they do: They attempt to dazzle their audiences with their sheer volume of knowledge on any given topic, most of it pulled directly from their asses. They spew it faster than you can Google it. Their goal with this information assault is to beat you into submission and assert their superior opinions. They base everything on information sources that you could not possibly have access to, which is sort of the equivalent of saying, "I have a girlfriend, but she lives in Canada."

What they're hiding: The fact that they're suffering from the intellectual equivalent of "penis envy."

THE CREDENTIAL FALSIFIERS

What they do: They claim to have unique life experiences or qualifications that you don't, which therefore validate their views and negate yours. For example, they may refer to their military training and combat experience when it turns out that all they ever did was play *World of Warcraft*.

What they're hiding: The fact that they're average and ill-informed.

THE "TRUTHINESS" TELLERS

What they do: They cling to the truths that come straight from their gut, rather than from reality. As defined by comedian Stephen Colbert, "truthiness" refers to an individual's preference for believing in what he or she wishes to be true rather than what is known to be true.

What they're hiding: Their utter terror of reality.

THE BULLSHIT ACOLYTES

What they do: They perpetuate right-wing spin through empty sloganeering and mindless repetition of GOP talking points crafted by Bill O'Reilly, Rush Limbaugh, Sean Hannity, and their many shrieking clones.

What they're hiding: That sheep vote Republican.

How to Trip Up a Bullshitter

Good bullshitters can be hard to spot, but you may be able to trip them up by their failure to answer basic questions or inability to support their claims. Next time you smell the stink, take the following steps:

1. Hit them with simple questions they probably won't be expecting, such as "How do you know that?"; "How can you prove that?"; or if it's something completely obvious: "So what you're saying is, the AP, CNN, *The Wall Street Journal*, and every other news agency in the world is wrong, and you, an unemployed, alcoholic Xbox player, are right?"

2. If you suspect they're just blindly spewing rhetoric or unthinkingly parroting right-wing spin, challenge them to provide specifics. For example, make them explain exactly how Obama's death panels are conspiring with FEMA to shoot puppies on the White House lawn, specifically how Democrats are plotting with Hollywood to turn everyone gay, or show how making health care more affordable is exactly what Hitler did.

3.   As they grasp to substantiate their claims, watch for telltale signs of lying, such as lack of eye contact, a scratch to the nose, or words coming out of their mouths forming sentences. Consider responses such as "I saw it on Glenn Beck's Web TV show," "I heard it at a GOP prayer rally," or "Because Bachmann said so" to be admissions that they see the world through bullshit-colored glasses.

4.   Call them on their deceit, show them where they went wrong, and suggest that they leave the bullshitting to trained professionals, like Sarah Palin armed with talking points, Rush Limbaugh armed with pain pills, or Rick Perry armed with… well, just armed.

How to Spot Logical Fallacies

If you've ever been part of an argument that feels disingenuous, grossly oversimplified, rigged against you, or which makes no earthly sense, then you've probably encountered a logical fallacy. They're the one-legged stools of faulty reasoning that conservatives rely on to prop up many of their ridiculous ideas.

Some conservatives deliberately use logical fallacies

to play manipulative mind games, while others may inadvertently stick a finger in the eye of reason. Whatever the case, learning to recognize common logical fallacies—and calling your opponent on them—will help you to immediately deflate many bogus lines of attack.

Or, if you're feeling Machiavellian, you can also deliberately use these techniques yourself to try and pull a fast one on an unwitting opponent. In fact, you may spot a few fallacies employed for comedic ends elsewhere in this book.

FALSE CHOICE

Offering only two options for consideration when there are clearly other valid choices.

Example: "Either you are with us, or you are with the terrorists." —*George W. Bush*

STRAW MAN

Oversimplifying, exaggerating, caricaturing, or otherwise misrepresenting your position without regard to fact. In doing this, your opponent sets up a figurative straw man that he can easily knock down to prove his point.

Example: "The America I know and love is not one in which my parents or my baby with Down syndrome will have to stand in front of Obama's 'death panel.'" —*Sarah Palin*

AD HOMINEM

Leveling a personal attack in an attempt to discredit an argument rather than addressing the argument itself.

Example: "It doesn't look like Michelle Obama follows her own nutritionary dietary advice. And then we hear that she's out eating ribs at 1500 calories a serving with 141 grams of fat...No, I'm trying to say that our first lady does not project the image of women that you might see on the cover of the *Sports Illustrated* swimsuit issue or of a woman Alex Rodriguez might date every six months or what have you." —*Rush Limbaugh, attempting to discredit Michelle Obama's anti-obesity campaign*

ARGUMENT FROM IGNORANCE

Attempting to argue that something is true because it has not been proven false, or vice versa.

Example: "I'll tell you why [religion is] not a scam, in my opinion. Tide goes in, tide goes out. Never a miscommunication. You can't explain that. You can't explain why the tide goes in." —*Bill O'Reilly, attempting to prove the existence of God*

SLIPPERY SLOPE

Leaping to wild, sometimes inexplicable conclusions— going, say, from step one to step two and then all the way to step ten without establishing any discernible connection. By using this kind of leapfrog logic, a person can come to any conclusion he damn well pleases.

Example: "If the Supreme Court says that you have the right to consensual sex within your home, then you have the right to bigamy, you have the right to polygamy, you have the right to incest, you have the right to adultery. You have the right to anything…that's not to pick on homosexuality. It's not, you know, man on child, man on dog, or whatever the case may be." —*ex-Sen. Rick Santorum (R-PA)*

REDUCTIO AD ABSURDUM

Attempting to disprove an opponent's position by taking it to an absurd conclusion.

Example: "So here you have Barack Obama going in and spending the money on embryonic stem cell research…Eugenics. In case you don't know what Eugenics led us to: the Final Solution. A master race! A perfect person…The stuff that we are facing is absolutely frightening." —*Glenn Beck*

APPEAL TO AUTHORITY

Invoking an authority figure—whether a politician, a famous person, or a so-called expert—to prove an argument rather than substantiating the argument itself.

Example: "There are hundreds and hundreds of scientists, many of them holding Nobel Prizes, who believe in intelligent design." —*Michele Bachmann, making a false argument from authority*

HASTY GENERALIZATION

Jumping to a far-reaching conclusion based on scant evidence or forming a stereotype based on a single flimsy example or two.

Example: "Liberals hate America, they hate flag-wavers, they hate abortion opponents, they hate all religions except Islam, post-9/11. Even Islamic terrorists don't hate America like liberals do. They don't have the energy. If they had that much energy, they'd have indoor plumbing by now." —*Ann Coulter*

SHIFTING THE BURDEN OF PROOF

Presenting an argument as commonly accepted truth, failing to support it with any evidence, and then forcing you to prove otherwise. This tactic is employed out of laziness or to mask the reality that the facts are not on your opponent's side.

Example: "I think the burden is on those people who think he didn't have weapons of mass destruction to tell the world where they are." —*Ari Fleischer, former* *press secretary for President George W. Bush, on Saddam Hussein's alleged WMDs*

FALSE CAUSE

This fallacy, known among logic buffs as *post hoc ergo propter hoc*, is based on the assertion that because one action or event occurs and is followed by another, the first must have caused the second.

Example: "We took the Bible and prayer out of public schools, and now we're having weekly shootings practically." —*Christine O'Donnell, failed Delaware GOP Senate candidate*

"If you can't beat them, arrange to have them beaten."

—**George Carlin**

How to Win When You Can't Win Them Over

As a passionate partisan who's determined to convert conservatives to your way of thinking, you want what anyone would want: to watch them grovel on their knees as they recant their beliefs and praise you for showing them the path to salvation.

But the reality is that you can do everything right, make flawless arguments, and still find yourself getting nowhere. Some conservatives are so unteachably ignorant, so self-righteously closed-minded, there is literally nothing you can say—or no legal torture method you can employ—to enlighten them. If you're planning to mix it up with conservatives who fit that profile, you'll need a blunter instrument than this book with which to beat them over the head.

Fortunately, there are a few other important ways in which you can still declare victory when you haven't won them over. You can unfurl your "Mission Accomplished" banner if you succeed in doing any of the following:

1. **Humiliate your opponent.** If you can undercut your opponent's arguments while making him look foolish in the process, you may not win a convert, but you can emancipate yourself—and perhaps a few grateful bystanders—from the spell of their bullshit.

2. **Sew your opponent with seeds of self-doubt.** If your opponent gives you everything he's got and

then finds himself trapped under the weight of his own inadequacy—making fruitless counter-arguments or being reduced to speechlessness—that's a good time to walk away. Let him fester in his own silent insufficiency. One day those seeds may bloom into giant flowers of debilitating self-doubt.

3.   **Win over the crowd.** When you're arguing with a conservative in front of other people—at a dinner party, for example—you can score a major victory simply by making superior arguments. Your goal is to appear more knowledgeable, more reasonable, and more logical, while exposing your opponent as ill-prepared, hypocritical, or simply clueless. Do that, and it doesn't matter whether you win over your adversary because you will have won the crowd.

4.   **Win a war of attrition.** You may not be able to bring someone around overnight, but with patience and persistence, and possibly with the help of enough alcohol, you may eventually break your opponents down and get them to admit the folly of their ways—or at least stop voting Republican.

★ **CHAPTER 5** ★

How to Win Friends While Antagonizing People

LUKE: Your thoughts betray you, Father. I feel the good in you, the conflict.

DARTH VADER: There is no conflict.

LUKE: You couldn't bring yourself to kill me before, and I don't believe you'll destroy me now.

DARTH VADER: You underestimate the power of the Dark Side. If you will not fight, then you will meet your destiny.

—Star Wars: Return of the Jedi

Everyone says you shouldn't argue politics in polite company. Wrong! Polite company is the best place to hone your combat skills. If you sit around waiting for impolite company to come along, your feeble skills will be no match for their pitchforks or their torches.

You have to start somewhere, so who better to prey on than your friends and loved ones or the guy in the next cubicle whose name you can't remember? Navigating these minefields, however, requires special training. To help you bait and baffle your adversaries (while avoiding interpersonal disaster), this chapter offers some essential "DOs" and "DON'Ts" for dealing with several potentially hazardous combat zones.

How to Survive Family Sparring Matches

For some families it's an annual ritual: Everyone is sitting around the dinner table, enjoying a lovely Thanksgiving meal and getting into the holiday spirit, when Uncle Blowhard says, "Speaking of things we have to be thankful for, every day I thank God for creating the Tea Party and all the good work they do." Cousin Tom takes the bait and says, "Where were those hypocritical morons when Bush was blowing stuff up, like our debt?" Pretty soon, the conversation descends into a back-and-forth volley of bitter pronouncements, like "I'd rather drink tea than Kool-Aid!" and "How about you drink a big steaming cup of shut the EFF up?" At which point chairs are pushed back and dishes are cleared, while your mother weeps quietly in the corner.

The thing about arguing with family is, you're in it for the long haul; they're as stuck with you as you are with them. That gives you a little more leeway, so everyone knows they can push the envelope further than they would in other situations. For that reason, a few basic rules apply.

★ **DO** openly boast to your uncle about the unemployment benefits you get and how there's really no incentive to get a job. Tell your aunt about how you and your girlfriend plan to have babies just so the government will take care of them. Later, excuse yourself, saying, "This medical marijuana isn't going to smoke itself."

★ **DO** crack jokes to disarm your opponents and lull them into a false sense of complacency. Keep an ample supply of alcohol at the ready; nobody bites the hand that gets them drunk. Or, an even better idea, ply them with coffee or Red Bull (people who are wired on caffeine are more susceptible to persuasion, according to an actual scientific study).

★ **DO** attempt to recruit impressionable family members to your side, particularly when they're young; for example, give your seven-year-old nephew a copy of the complete *Star Wars* saga on Blu-ray and explain how Jedis are Democrats and the evil Sith Lords are Republicans—as identified by their blue and red light sabers. This tactic is referred to as "the old liberal mind trick."

★ **DO** quote the Bible when arguing with your religious relatives, as beating zealots with their own stick can be a blissful religious experience. Be sure to bring up the parts they choose to gloss over, like "love thy neighbor," "the meek shall inherit the Earth," and "thou shall not molest thine underage page." Whenever they refer to something as an "abomination," just respond with "So is eating shellfish, but that didn't slow you down at Red Lobster last week." Or, quiz them on why they didn't stone Uncle Max when he left Aunt Ellen for his secretary.

★ **DON'T** let Uncle Blowhard hold the dinner table hostage. Fact-check him right then and there using your smart phone or iPad. Counter him point-for-point, fire off contradictory statistics, and inform him he scored a "Pants on Fire" on PolitiFact's Truth-O-Meter test. Remember, conservatives hate facts. They get in the way of sweeping generalizations. It's like sunlight to a vampire.

★ **DON'T** proselytize to your children about your politics; they'll just rebel. First they'll start experimenting by reading conservative blogs (also known as "gateway blogs"). Then they'll progress to binge use of GOP talking points at weekend social gatherings. Before you know it they'll have developed a habitual dependency on conservative dogma, for which there may be no rehabilitation. (See: Carlson, Tucker)

★ **DON'T** try to get in the last word with a conservative loved one at his or her own funeral. It comes off as insensitive to stand over a deceased conservative saying, "I bet you wish you'd had universal health care now," "Guess that estate tax isn't so important where you're going," or "Let me know what Jesus has to say about trickle-down economics when you're panhandling in hell."

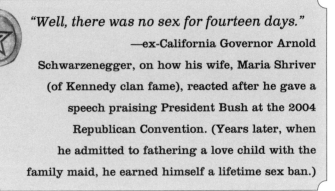

"Well, there was no sex for fourteen days."

—ex-California Governor Arnold Schwarzenegger, on how his wife, Maria Shriver (of Kennedy clan fame), reacted after he gave a speech praising President Bush at the 2004 Republican Convention. (Years later, when he admitted to fathering a love child with the family maid, he earned himself a lifetime sex ban.)

What to Do If You're Sleeping with the Enemy

Love makes people do crazy things, and chief among them is dating (or even marrying) your political enemy. Many households have their own partisan divides. He listens to Rush Limbaugh; she listens to NPR. He votes for the candidate he'd like to drink beer with; she goes with the person she'd rather trust performing brain surgery. He's James Carville, the serpent-headed Democratic strategist known as the Ragin' Cajun; she's Mary Matalin, the sharp-tongued Republican strategist who helped Dick Cheney rule the galaxy.

Some mixed couples manage to coexist in a state of harmony. For others, it ends with a restraining order. Consider the case of one couple in Georgia who made headlines after the woman informed her boyfriend, a Marine recruit, that she was leaving him *and* voting for John Kerry back in 2004. That's when he tried to stab her repeatedly with a screwdriver. "You'll never live to see the election," he told her before officers subdued him with a Taser.

To help you remain faithful to both your beliefs and your significant other (while keeping yourself out of jail), here are a few pointers.

- ★ **DO** keep political banter light. Ask yourself WWJSD (What Would Jon Stewart Do?) and try to maintain a sense of ironic self-detachment.
- ★ **DO** consider withholding sex to make a political point. If that doesn't work, women can try withholding gadgets or restricting his PlayStation or TiVo privileges. (Note: This suggestion may be an impossible task for males to pull off. Only make these threats if you are absolutely certain you can go through with it. If you are bluffing, your bluff will be called! Expect your female partner to look hotter than she has ever looked and offer to do things to you sexually that you are going to have to Google. All this while she's unboxing the latest *Call of Duty* game.)

★ **DO** agree on a safe word to signal when you've reached your limit, like people do with S&M; if he's extolling the virtues of repealing the capital gains tax and you just can't take it anymore, shout out "eight ball," "bananas," or "Bernanke" and take a time-out.

★ **DO** go to the farmers' market together. Farmers are the salt of the earth, and no conservative worth his weight in tax cuts could disrespect a farmer. On the other hand, the people who go to the farmers' markets are the biggest bunch of Birkenstock-wearing, ponytail-having, reusable-hemp-bag-carrying neo-hippies around. This should make his head explode.

★ **DON'T** engage in any sort of political discussion with your opposite-ideological partner if you're hoping to get laid afterward. Wait until after sex. Two and a half minutes is not going to kill you. Remember, if you're having sex correctly, you won't have the energy for the argument to get out of hand. (If perchance the sex was unprotected, now would be a good time to discuss a woman's right to choose.)

★ **DON'T** resort to amateurish passive-aggressive behavior, such as lining the birdcage with your honey's absentee ballot. Instead, take it up a notch—host a PETA party at the house and release his prized bird back to nature.

★ **DON'T** spell-check your partner's protest signs before she walks out the door to a Tea Party rally. They're supposed to be filled with spelling and grammatical errors. It's how they identify themselves to one another as authentic Tea Partiers. It's the same way a mama grizzly can tell her cubs by their smell. Besides, she won't believe you anyway, since Tea Partiers know spelling to be a socialist plot, along with math, science, and all other fields of study that could accidentally lead to learning.

★ **DON'T** kid yourself; if you discover a robe, a hood, and a stockpile of ammunition, pack up the kids and head for the nearest blue state. You won't be able to "work it out." That will have to be done by the FBI negotiators during the standoff.

How to Manage Workplace Squabbles

During the course of their adult lives, most Americans are doomed to spend about one-third of their waking hours toiling in the workplace. Whether you're looking for a political argument or not, sooner or later, you're bound to find yourself mixing it up with that conservative colleague who's always spouting off about how the office health plan wouldn't be so expensive if it weren't for "Obamacare" or griping about the high cost of gas because tree-hugging liberals won't let us drill in the oil-rich playgrounds of our nation's public schools.

Because workplace arguments can be a serious occupational hazard, here are some tips that will help you serve your partisan cause while holding on to your job at the same time.

★ **DO** turn a difference of opinion into a friendly wager. If you win a bet about Democrats prevailing in the upcoming election, for example, your coworker has to agree to travel the country following Phish on tour. If you lose, you agree to follow Ted Nugent. (Don't lose!)

★ **DO** form alliances with like-minded colleagues; a coordinated assault around the water cooler by a coalition of the willing is always better than going it alone. It will also make that sit-in you have planned in the IT department more effective. If you're just sitting there by yourself, they'll think you're there for IT help, rather than protesting the oppressive firewall they created that restricts you from watching *Daily Show* and Colbert clips at work.

★ **DO** leverage your position to impose your views on others. If you are in the IT department, set office passwords to things like "goobama," "legalize-weed," "taxhikesfortherich!" or "suckitboehner."

★ **DO** consider being a double agent; convince a conservative colleague that you're actually a conservative too and win his or her trust. This may involve doing some unspeakable acts, such as reading a book by Ann Coulter or eating an endangered condor for lunch. Then at a crucial moment—say, right before Election Day—express your total disillusionment with the Republican Party and convince your colleague to join you in abandoning ship.

★ **DON'T** get into a political spat with your boss unless you have some sort of leverage, like illicit intern photos or stock manipulation documents. In that case, have a go at it: nothing is more fun than blackmailing your boss into wearing a "Nailin' Palin" muscle-T on casual Friday.

★ **DON'T** be a stalker, like that guy in accounting with bad breath who's always cornering people, ranting about the evils of the military industrial complex, and trying to get you to read his MySpace blog; no one likes that guy. That's why they don't tell him MySpace is a dead social network.

★ **DON'T** plaster your workspace with annoying propaganda or signage (e.g., stickers that say "U.S. out of my uterus"—especially if you don't have a uterus—or that photo of you and Dennis Kucinich writhing in the mud at Burning Man). It signals you're either desperate for attention or huffing liquid paper. In either case, your coworkers will avoid you.

"They say, 'It's not whether you win or lose, it's how you play the game.' That's why I play every sport with a baseball bat—the other boxer never sees it coming."

—**Stephen Colbert**

How to Clash with Perfect Strangers

A few days after the 2004 presidential election, a pugnacious liberal posted the following anonymous message on craigslist.org in Washington, D.C.: "I would like to fight a Bush supporter to vent my anger. If you are one, [and] have a fiery streak, please contact me so we can meet and physically fight. I would like to beat the shit out of you."

Another craigslist poster offered a similar proposition: "Any of you Republicans want to fight? Street brawl, bodies only, no weapons. I will not be merciful. I'm sick of this tough-guy shit. Let's see what you got."

Going around and picking fights with strangers is generally not recommended. However, there are a few situations where *verbally* mixing it up with strangers may be warranted, perhaps even imperative. Here are a few guidelines.

★ **DO** feel free to mix it up with petition gatherers, pamphleteers, and other partisan stalkers; the longer you hold them hostage, the less time they'll have to disperse their propaganda. In fact, take as much paraphernalia as they're willing to hand out to you. Then, when you're closing the door or walking away, say loud enough for them to hear, "I can't wait to recycle all this stuff and save a tree!"

★ **DO** feel free to wear your "My guy killed Bin Laden, what did your guy do?" T-shirt while strolling the mall. When somebody inevitably says that he didn't actually pull the trigger, you can reply with, "Well, he didn't fire you from your job, but that doesn't stop you from blaming him."

★ **DO** feel free to track down the Republicans responsible for the annoying and incessant "robo-calls" you received telling you that the Democrat on the ballot drinks the blood of children. Find the home phone numbers for anyone involved, anonymously post them on every liberal blog, sit back, and enjoy the turn of the karmic wheel.

★ **DON'T** antagonize anyone who may be able to take advantage of you in a compromising situation, such as your hairstylist, skydiving instructor, proctologist, tattoo artist, or the guy making your burrito.

★ **DON'T** get into an argument with the conservative sitting next to you on an airplane. At some point in every argument with a conservative you will be called a terrorist, and an airplane is the last place you want to be when that happens. And worse, you'll have no exit strategy.

★ **DON'T** attempt to enter a political discussion with anyone while you are high on marijuana. Nothing undermines your credibility like being called a liberal hippie stoner when you *are* a liberal hippie stoner. If you are a hippie stoner, and you made it this far into the book, congratulations!

★ **DON'T** pick a fight without first taking stock of your opponent and your surroundings. Is your opponent alone or part of a large group? Are you in an enclosed area like a dark alley? Does your opponent's leather vest say either "Hell's" or "Angels"? Did your opponent just come out of a dojo, shooting range, or meth lab? If the answer to any of these questions is yes, abort! Remember, discretion is the better part of valor and self-preservation.

How to Argue Politics on Facebook and Twitter

Popular social media sites like Facebook and Twitter have done more than just revolutionize the way we stalk old flames or tend to virtual crops; they've also pioneered entirely new ways to win or lose political arguments.

You're bound to have at least a few hardcore conservatives among your friends or followers, which means that, sooner or later, you're going to see the unwelcome sight of someone pasting Fox News talking points into his or her status updates or re-tweeting the latest refudiations from @SarahPalinUSA. Butting heads through these kinds of social media interactions (in what amounts to a room full of all your friends) is fraught with great danger, but also great opportunity, which is why some unique DOs and DON'Ts apply.

★ **DO** link or share anything that uses biting humor to make a political point, such as clips from *The Daily Show* or *The Colbert Report*, witty quips from comedians, political cartoons, or funny images (you can find lots of fresh fodder at facebook.com/politicalhumor). If a conservative reacts with hostility, just accuse him of not being able to take a joke, and you'll make him look like a humorless schmuck.

★ **DO** enlist other Facebook friends to engage in a virtual sneak attack. You can start the fun by updating your status with provocative statements that will drive your opponents crazy, like how you love Jesus because he was a liberal Jew who hung out with hookers. If a conservative takes the bait, privately message your friends and get them to swarm on him like wild dogs on a piece of meat. By the time he's finished reading the tenth successive post illustrating why he's both wrong and an idiot, he'll never know what hit him.

★ **DO** create intentionally misleading Twitter identities for evil conservatives like @crazyeyesbachmann, @MitMeister, or @Caintrain2012 and then post things that are closer to the truth than the actual fluff they post. For instance: "@Caintrain2012: Hey immigrants, just kidding about electrified border fence, dead serious about the packs of rabid Dobermans."

★ **DO** feel free to tweet outlandish statements about your opponents, as long as you follow it up with the hashtag "justsaying" (#justsaying). This absolves you of any responsibility for whatever you attribute to that individual because you were "justsaying" that. So if you say, "No way Newt's head could be that large if he didn't feast on babies #justsaying," or "@RickSantorum is way too homophobic to not be gay #justsaying," or "John Boehner is orange cause he gets hummers from orangutans #justsaying," then your opponent can't get mad at you because you remembered to use the #justsaying hashtag.

★ **DON'T** take the bait when somebody you know on Facebook attempts to get a rise out of his lefty friends by spewing so called "facts" about liberals trying to promote death panels and offering free abortions with your next mandatory gay marriage. If his post is met with crickets, not only will he look like a loser, he'll also be punished by Facebook's algorithm for failing to elicit interaction, and fewer and fewer people will see his posts over time. You win by silence and by default. God bless Mark Zuckerberg.

★ **DON'T** "like" your own posts or comments. It just makes you look like an insecure egomaniac or an idiot who hit the wrong button. Instead, create a fake account, and then you'll have your own personal wingman who can like everything you say, and post fawning comments such as, "You are SO insightful," "You go girl!" or "I hope everybody reads this because this is the smartest thing anyone has ever said about Mitt Romney's magic underwear."

★ **DON'T** pay to have millions of fake Twitter followers and then brag about them as your credential for being president. (See Gingrich, Newt)

★ **DON'T** use cutesy lingo like IMHO (in my humble opinion) on Twitter. If you say it, we know it's your opinion, and if you are broadcasting it on Twitter, it's probably not sincerely humble. Also avoid LOL or LMAO at your own tweets—we'll be the judge of that, thank you. In real life if you have to laugh out loud at your own jokes to let people know they're funny, you just look like a moron.

★ **DON'T** unfriend, block, or completely hide the updates from your crazy right-winger friends, because you'll be missing out on the chance to bait and mock them. Instead, create a special list for these people. Call it something like "Monkeys in a Barrel." Think of it as your own private window to the loony bin. Check it periodically to see how the right is "thinking," or to test out new lines of attack. Or, if you're having a crappy day, just rip into them. It's twenty-four-hour free cathartic therapy and about the only free health care you'll get from conservatives.

★   **DON'T** drink and tweet. When you come home after a long night of revelry, it may be tempting to respond to a right-wing jab, but don't do it. You won't be at your sharpest and it undermines your credibility when you tweet things like "Tax the rich, except my good friend Jack Daniels" or "Bachmann-Palin would be a bad ticket but good three-way." Remember, Twitter is a public medium and once you press "send," it's out there. You don't want to wake up in the morning to find that your response to a tweet on the validity of supply side economics was a two-word tweet that said "suck it," accompanied by an uncensored photo of your junk.

How to Properly Engage in Internet Flame Wars

If you've never been denounced as a bedwetting, fascist, crack-addicted, terrorist crybaby by dozens of people you've never met, you've never experienced the joys of an Internet flame war. For the uninitiated, here's a recap of every political debate ever held in an online political forum or the comments section of various blogs and news sites, courtesy of Bill Maher:

"'Obama is a socialist.' 'Oh yeah, Bush is a war criminal, fag.' 'Who you calling a fag, faggot?' The end. And then of course, someone chimes in with 'Ron Paul 2012,' and they call that guy a fag. And then, I can't help myself, so I type, 'Gentlemen, gentlemen, please! This is a porn site!'"

The upside to engaging in Internet flame wars is (1) you get to deploy all the anti-conservative epithets and denunciations that have been swirling in your mind (see After-*Words*: 125,000 Ways to Insult Conservatives); and (2) it's generally all anonymous, which means there's no need to lose any sleep over the taunts or fatwas that will inevitably be issued against you.

If you plan to get involved in a flame war, here are a few things to keep in mind. Note that some of these tips run counter to the advice offered elsewhere in the book. That's the whole point of flame wars. They're anonymous, so normal rules of decorum need not apply.

★　**DO** tell anyone who calls you a Nazi that they've automatically lost the argument for violating Godwin's Law of Nazi Analogies, which says that in any sufficiently long Internet discussion, someone will eventually compare his or her opponent to Nazis or Hitler. Be sure to make this point while calling your opponent everything short of a Nazi (i.e., digital brownshirt, cyber jihadist, fascist troll, and, where appropriate, batshit-crazy, genocidal douche bag).

★ **DO** feel free to invent your own facts. If pressed for evidence, take a page out of the Sarah Palin/ Michelle Bachmann playbook and simply create your own Wikipedia entry to support your made-up arguments. The Internet is overflowing with incorrect information; what's a little more going to hurt?

★ **DO** occasionally misrepresent yourself to play mind games with your opponent. You're no longer a liberal who wants to raise taxes on the rich. You're now a conservative hedge fund manager who supports the idea. You're no longer a liberal who believes in evolution. You're now a right-wing evangelical Christian who has come to see the light. You're no longer a liberal who believes in gay marriage. You're now Rick Santorum and have become a convert to the cause after Googling your name and becoming oddly intrigued.

★   **DO** take personal offense to everything you can, even if it's not personal. Explain, for example, that you lost an arm, a leg, and an eye in the War on Christmas and you're outraged by his callous insensitivity. Tell him that somewhere terrorists are reading his posts and high-fiving each other because they know they've won.

★   **DO** pretend to be an expert on whatever subject matter you're arguing, as a way of pulling rank and trumping your opponent. If you're arguing taxes, say you're a Nobel prize-winning economist. If you're arguing about terrorism, say you're a member of Seal Team 6. If you're arguing with a Bible-thumper, tell them you're God and to stop putting words in your mouth.

★   **DO** demonstrate that you are on the cutting edge of Internet discourse by using expletives such as "asshat," "derp," and "dill weed." Bonus points: If you use the number "3" instead of the letter "e" and "P" in place of "O," you'll confuse the piss out of them and let them know they've been "Pwn3d! LOL!"

★   **DON'T** ever defend your own arguments. That's a rookie mistake and a waste of your time. Instead, keep your opponent constantly on the defensive. For example, after you've stated that conservatives have a plan to euthanize the elderly, don't respond to their demands for proof; simply move on to your next attack, arguing that Ronald Reagan was a notorious cross-dresser. Put the onus on them to disprove everything you're saying. If they hit Caps Lock and start shouting at you, consider that a win. You have helped create a safe outlet for their rage, and that's one less kitten they're likely to torture.

★ **DON'T** ever provide any real information about yourself. Facebook is doing enough of that already and you don't need any more personal info on the Internet. Besides, it's more fun to pretend to be someone you're not—a mid-level Homeland Security official, for example, who is carefully monitoring everything they're saying.

★ **DON'T** get overly worked up or spend too much time flaming. You are never going to "win" the argument. In the annals of Internet flame wars, not once has anyone walked away from the computer saying, "You know, lefty69 was right. Supply-side economics has proven ineffective and perhaps it is time we try a Keynesian approach." The goal is not to "win"; it's to make the other guy as angry as possible. If you get angry or worked up, you lose.

★ **DON'T** limit yourself to just one identity, make sure to have several. The more the merrier. Use an entire online ensemble to agree with you and trash your opponent. It may feel a little like cheating, but if your opponent thinks the entire Internet is run by liberals, it may keep him off the Internet and out of your life.

CHAPTER 6

Kick-Ass Comebacks to Conservative Nonsense

"Yeah, well, you know, that's just like, uh, your opinion man."

—The Dude in *The Big Lebowski*.

Always bet on The Dude.

Now that you're primed for battle, it's time to get down and dirty and argue the issues. Conservatives mindlessly spew so many ludicrous talking points that are unsupported by facts and common sense, it's hard to rebut them all. But we present here a bundle of kick-ass comebacks to common right-wing ridiculousness you're likely to encounter.

Your goal is to seize control and reframe the debate to your advantage through all necessary means: throw inconvenient facts in their faces, stump them with pointed questions, expose their ignorance, beat them in a battle of wits, or quote somebody famous or funny to help make your point.

Keep in mind there's no such thing as a magical retort that will leave your opponent flattened as you triumphantly spike the ball in the end zone. But think of these as winning openers that will put you in a better position to win—or at least temporarily shut them up as they scramble to pull more drivel from the shallow recesses of their logic-resistant, fact-allergic brains.

How to Argue with an Obamaphobe

When they say: Obama has done nothing.

You say: He killed Osama, toppled Gaddafi, ended the Iraq war, is drawing the Afghanistan war to a close (like he said he would), enacted health care reform (after other politicians spent fifty years just talking about it), signed financial reform legislation ending corrupt banking practices, repealed the military's senseless "Don't Ask, Don't Tell" policy, didn't screw up a hurricane, prevented a second Great Depression, AND brought back *Arrested Development*. You're welcome, America.

When they say: Obama is destroying America.
You say: But you just said he's done nothing. Which is it?

When they say: Obama had four years in office and made everything worse.
You say: Let's remember that Bush basically handed Obama the keys to a burning house. We were losing hundreds of thousands of jobs every month, but Obama brought us back from the brink. Rome wasn't built in a day, and you don't fix a giant economic calamity overnight. Why do Republicans expect Obama to clean up the mess they made in about half the time it took for them to fuck everything up?

When they say: If Obama has been truly honest about his identity, how come one in five Americans still believe he's a Muslim?
You say: One in five Americans also believe in alien

abductions, can't find the U.S. on a map, and think George W. Bush was a great president.

When they say: Obama dug us into a big economic hole.

You say: Let's let Elizabeth Warren (Democratic Senate candidate from Massachusetts) field this one: "We got into this hole because of $1 trillion spent on tax cuts for the rich under George W. Bush. We got into this mess because of $2 trillion spent on two wars that were put on a credit card for our children and grandchildren to pay off. And we got into this hole because of $1 trillion Republicans spent on a Medicare drug program that was not paid for and was 40 percent more expensive than it needed to be because it was a giveaway to the drug companies. So part of the way you fix this problem is 'don't do those things'!"

When they say: I'm mad as hell about Obama's fiscal irresponsibility.

You say: Where were you during the eight years when Bush and Republicans exploded the deficit and set record levels of spending? Where was your outrage then? Where were your tricornered hats and fifes when your guys gave away our surplus and invaded the wrong country in an unfunded war? You applauded Dick Cheney when he said, "Reagan proved deficits don't matter." But now you're outraged? Admit it, you're only really mad because there's a Democrat in office who is actually taking steps to fix the economy, whipping terrorists, and can correctly pronounce the word "nuclear."

When they say: But Obama bailed out all the banks with that TARP program.

You say: Somebody must have spiked your tea, because that was George W.'s doing. But the drinking does explain the funny hats, misspelled signs, and belligerent attitudes. You should probably call your sponsor.

When they say: If Obama is for it, I'm against it.

You say: This is why Republican positions no longer make any sense. They keep opposing things they were once for—like middle class tax cuts, infrastructure spending, nuclear treaties, and reason-based thought. As Keith Olbermann once noted, "If Obama came out in favor of breathing, Republicans would hold their breath. And then when the cameras were off, they would seek government-supplied oxygen."

When they say: Obama is appeasing terrorists.

You say: Let's let Obama answer this one himself: "Ask Osama bin Laden and the twenty-two out of thirty top al Qaeda leaders who have been taken off the field whether I engage in appeasement—or whoever's left out there, ask them about that."

When they say: Obama doesn't know how to defend America.

You say: Let's see. Republicans controlled the White House, Congress, and the entire national security apparatus on the day we suffered the worst terrorist attack in American history. They also controlled everything when they launched two ineffectual wars, one of them completely phony. If that's how you define safe, great, but I'll go with the guy who actually killed bin Laden and doesn't think "yee-haw" is a foreign policy doctrine.

When they say: How do we know the birth certificate Obama showed us wasn't a fake?

You say: How do we know Obama was even born? How do we know he isn't a hologram or some kind of CGI creation of Hollywood liberals? Forget about the birth certificate already. Can anyone show us Sarah

Palin's high school diploma? Or how about Michelle Bachmann's release papers from the insane asylum?

"First they ignore you, then they laugh at you, then they fight you, then you win."

—**Gandhi**

How to Argue with Economic Ignoramuses

When they say: Liberals are waging class warfare!

You say: It's not class warfare to ask a hedge fund manager to pay the same tax rate as a teacher. As Warren Buffet once said, "There's class warfare, all right, but it's my class, the rich class, that's making war, and we're winning."

When they say: Democrats have exploded the national debt.

You say: It's a fact that about 70 percent of the recent U.S. debt was accumulated during the Republican presidential terms. If you think Obama is a socialist because of the debt he's added, that would make George W. Bush Chairman Mao and Ronald Reagan Karl Marx.

When they say: The best way to create jobs is to cut taxes.

You say: Been there, done that, doesn't work. Bush cut taxes for eight years and we ended up with the lowest period of job creation in the post World War II-era. As Stephen Colbert explained, "Yes, job creators like me need low taxes so we can continue to create jobs. Just look at history. In 1995, the effective tax rate paid by millionaires was 30.4%. By 2009, it had dropped to 22.4%. And over that same period, unemployment plummeted from 5.6% all the way down to 9.3%. But folks, I promise, there are more jobs coming. Just be patient. We job creators are like a slot machine. If you just keep pumping in tax cuts, eventually we're gonna pay off. You can't quit now, you've got us all warmed up."

When they say: Government needs to get out of the way so the rich can help our economy thrive.

You say: Elizabeth Warren put it best: "There is nobody in this country who got rich on his own. Nobody. You built a factory out there—good for you. You moved your goods to market on the roads the rest of us paid for. You hired workers the rest of us paid to educate. You were safe in your factory because of police forces and fire forces that the rest of us paid for. You didn't have to worry that marauding bands would come and seize everything at your factory… Look, you built a factory and it turned into something terrific or a great idea—God bless! Keep a big hunk of it. But part of the underlying social contract is you take a hunk of that and pay forward for the next kid who comes along."

When they say: Eliminating tax loopholes is just as bad as raising taxes.

You say: I'm with the president who said, "We're going to close the unproductive tax loopholes that allow some of the truly wealthy to avoid paying their fair share," because "in practice they sometimes made it possible for millionaires to pay nothing, while a bus driver was paying 10 percent of his salary, and that's crazy." No, it wasn't Obama who said that; it was Ronald Reagan!

When they say: Rich people are job creators.

You say: Exhibit A for why that's bullshit: The Situation from *Jersey Shore*. As Bill Maher pointed out, "The

Situation made $5 million dollars last year, and if he has to pay a little more in taxes, it won't mean he's creating fewer jobs. It will mean a tiny fraction of his money actually pays for the government that works to keep him alive. The EPA that contains his oil runoff. The Postal Service that delivers his body wax. The Bureau of Weights and Measures who weigh his dumbbells. The Centers for Disease Control that provides a steady supply of penicillin. And the military, who keep the Taliban away. Because if a single human proves that America is asking for it, you're looking at him."

When they say: CEOs deserve their pay. We need to pay them top dollar to get top talent.

You say: "We have got to pay those bailed-out firm CEOs top-dollar! Otherwise those companies could wind up being run by a couple of jackasses who fuck things up so royally it torpedoes the entire global economy. Would you want that to happen?"
—*Jon Stewart*

When they say: Corporations are people.

You say: If corporations are people, show us their birth certificates.

When they say: Corporations already pay enough taxes. We need to cut corporate taxes.

You say: There were thirty-seven giant corporations that paid zero taxes in 2010. Guess what? You paid more taxes than companies like General Electric, Boeing, Verizon, Wells Fargo, and DuPont *combined.* Tell me, how much lower than zero do you think their corporate taxes should be?

When they say: Forty-seven percent of Americans don't pay taxes! They're freeloaders!

You say: That's a distortion of reality. They pay no federal tax, but they pay payroll taxes, state and local taxes, property taxes, gas taxes, excise taxes, and much more. But let me get this straight, you're a Republican who's against raising taxes, but you want to *raise taxes* on these 47 percent? The so-called 47 percent includes such "freeloaders" as people who are too old to work, full-time students, kids, the disabled, the long-term unemployed, and a substantial number of jailed former congressmen. So I'm a little fuzzy on your math. Do you go around asking homeless guys to pay your mortgage? You can't tax broke.

"Did you know that the words 'race car' spelled backwards still spells 'race car'? That 'eat' is the only word that, if you take the 1st letter and move it to the last, spells its past tense, 'ate'?

"And if you rearrange the letters in 'so-called tea party Republicans,' and add just a few more letters, it spells: 'Shut the hell up you free-loading, progress-blocking, benefit-grabbing, resource-sucking, violent, hypo-critical a-holes, and face the fact that you nearly wrecked the country under Bush.'

"Isn't that interesting?"

—An email that made the rounds in 2010

How to Taunt a Tea Partier

When they say: Tea Partiers are keeping it real.

You say: Gotta love those Tea Partiers. They chant "USA, USA" while waving a Confederate flag. They oppose social programs, while cashing Social Security checks and receiving Medicare benefits. They say they're pro-life, and yet they're pro-guns, pro-death penalty, pro-war, and anti-health-care.

They call Obama a dictator for trying to raise taxes on the rich, even though Reagan raised taxes on everyone a dozen times. They hate big government telling them what to do, and then insist on banning abortion, banning gay marriage, and drug testing people on welfare. Way to keep it real. *(from the "Tea Party Ted" Internet meme)*

When they say: We Tea Partiers are freedom fighters just like the Founding Fathers.

You say: To quote Bill Maher: "While you idolize the Founding Fathers and dress up like them, and smell like them, I think it's pretty clear that the Founding Fathers would have hated your guts. And what's more, you would've hated them. They were everything you despise. They studied science, read Plato, hung out in Paris, and thought the Bible was mostly bullshit."

When they say: Down with taxes!

You say: I hate taxes, too, but I like schools, roads, firefighters, police officers, hospitals, paramedics, soldiers, sailors, airmen, clean air, clean water, safe food, child protection, safe products, space exploration, universities, museums, science, criminal

justice, medical research, tunnels, bridges, flood
defenses, and national parks, so I save my bitching
for important stuff like the designated hitter rule.
(from PunditKitchen.com)

When they say: Down with government!

You say: "All the Tea Party people who think no government is a good idea should spend a week in Somalia
or Wisconsin." —*Andy Borowitz*

When they say: Keep the government's hands off my
Medicare! (a common chant at Tea Party rallies)

You say: That's like saying, "Don't let McDonald's start
serving hamburgers!"

When they say: We Tea Partiers are fighting for liberty.

You say: Actually, you are fighting for the Koch brothers and Richard Mellon Scaife, who are funding your
tea parties and whose real goal is unaccountable
private power. You're fighting for BP's right to coat
your crawfish with oil. You are fighting for health
insurance companies' right to call your C-section a
preexisting condition and deny you coverage. You
are fighting for the right of food makers to write
their own safety rules, because what better way to

celebrate liberty than with a little *Listeria* on your cantaloupe? But those billionaires really appreciate your hard work. Once they're done destroying the middle class and the environment, maybe you can mow their lawn.

When they say: We must go back and uphold the original Constitution.

You say: So I guess that means that only white male property owners will be able to vote. I'll tell your wife, but you have to tell all the black people that they are now only three-fifths of a person. Good luck, Mr. Constitution.

When they say: Liberals have turned us into a nation of slaves.

You say: Really? You don't get paid for your work? You're forced to toil in fields for eighteen hours a day with barely any food or water? You're beaten when you step out of line? You are forcibly separated from your family? Wow, I didn't realize you had it so bad. Hey, is that the new iPhone you're using?

When they say: I'm teabagging for Jesus.

You say: I'm pretty sure he didn't swing that way.

When they say: "*Youth in Asia* Will Kill Your Grandma," "No *Pubic* Option!," "Remember *descent* is the highest form of patriotism," "Make English America's *Offical* Language," or "Thank you Fox News for keeping us *infromed*" (all actual misspelled protest signs seen at Tea Party rallies)

You say: You are entitled to your own opinion, but not your own spelling.

"I said, 'Because I believe that people should be able to share their life with whomever they want and the role of government is to administer that contract that they agree to enter into.' And he stopped and said, 'But they're changing the definition of marriage.' And I said, 'Don't get so excited about this marriage stuff.' I said, 'Think about this, we just met, you and I right here at the stoplight. You stuck your head in the window of my car. Do you know tomorrow we could go to City Hall, we could apply for a marriage license, and we could get married, and nobody there will ask us about the quality of our relationship or whether we've been committed to

> *each other or any of those things? They will issue that marriage license and we can get married.' And he said, 'Yes, that's true.' I said, 'Do you think we're ready for that kind of commitment?' And he stopped and he said, 'I see your point.'"*
>
> —New York State Senator Diane Savino (D), recounting a story about a confrontation she had with a man at a stoplight, who asked her why she was voting for New York's gay marriage bill

How to Clash with Clueless Conservatives on Hot-Button Issues

When they say: Gay marriage will lead to dog marriage.
You say: "Gay marriage will not lead to dog marriage. It's not a slippery slope to rampant interspecies coupling. When women got the right to vote, it didn't lead to hamsters voting. No court has extended the equal protection clause to salmon." —*Bill Maher*

When they say: Gay marriage will weaken straight marriage.
You say: Gay people just want one marriage. It's not like they're Newt Gingrich or anything.

When they say: Health-care reform is fascism! It's socialism! It's tyranny!

You say: What's so ironic about the health-care reform you so adamantly oppose is that it would help you get the Prozac you so desperately need. —*Bill Maher, paraphrased*

When they say: Obamacare is a government takeover that will lead to socialized medicine.

You say: Without Obamacare, insurance companies can just dump the uninsurable on the government. Then they get thrown on Medicaid or other taxpayer-dime services, which are basically socialized medicine programs. So by being against Obamacare, *you* are supporting socialized medicine. You sick Commie bastard!

When they say: What have unions ever given us?

You say: Basically nothing, unless you count maternity leave. And weekends off. And workers' comp. Oh, and fair wages, sick days, ending discrimination, ending child labor, fighting for employer-based health coverage, and protection for whistleblowers. But that's it! *(from MoveOn.org)*

When they say: Abstinence education works.

You say: Right, it worked really well in places like Texas, where they now have one of the highest teen birth rates in the nation. They also tried it in Alaska, in Sarah Palin's house, where it was so effective that not only did daughter Bristol famously become a teen mom, she also thought, "Hey, this abstinence stuff works so well, I gotta teach it to others! For money!" Of course, we all know the real reason why conservatives love abstinence education. They believe that children born of ignorance are more likely to grow up and vote Republican.

When they say: Evolution is a myth.

You say: Evolution is a fact, backed by unanimous scientific consensus. But I'll be honest, watching all those Tea Party clowns parade around in their silly costumes with tea bags dangling everywhere from their ears to their nipples, carrying signs that say "Obama is a fascist socialist Marxist Maoist Kenyan Nazi," I'm beginning to have my doubts too.

When they say: Global warming is not real.

You say: There's no credible scientist who refutes the overwhelming evidence that climate change is man-made. Even Richard Muller, a skeptic funded by the Koch brothers to disprove global warming, came around and declared that it's real. Let's go with what Jon Huntsman (the only GOP presidential candidate who ever made a nickel's worth of sense) said: "I'm not a meteorologist. All I know is 90 percent of the scientists say climate change is occurring. If 90 percent of the oncology community said something was causing cancer we'd listen to them." Of course, that's probably overestimating conservatives; they wouldn't listen to the oncologists either.

When they say: What if we take action on global warming and it's just a big hoax?

You say: Then we'll have achieved energy independence, created green jobs, developed livable cities, cultivated renewable resources, fostered sustainability, preserved the rainforests, cleaned up our air, made our children healthier, and created a better world for nothing. (*from cartoonist Joel Pett*)

When they say: We have to get rid of the EPA. It's killing jobs.

You say: I'll agree to shutting down the Environmental Protection Agency as soon as you eat a BP tar ball. You can't trust the air and water our children breathe to the same people who brought you the Exxon Valdez spill, the Massey Energy mining disaster, and the Three Mile Island meltdown. The only reason to ban the EPA would be in the hope that our next generation gets cool toxic mutant powers.

When they say: The way to achieve energy independence is to "Drill, Baby, Drill!"

You say: That brings to mind what H. L. Mencken once said: "For every complex problem, there is an answer that is clear, simple, and wrong."

When they say: You should be the spokesman for Occupy Wall Street. Better go get yourself a bongo drum.

You say: "If I am the spokesman for all the people who think we should not have 24 million people in this country who can't find a full time job; that we should not have 50 million people who can't see a doctor when they're sick; that we shouldn't have 47 million people in this country who need government help to feed themselves; and we shouldn't have 15 million families who owe more on their mortgage than the value of their homes, OK, I'll be that spokesman." —*Alan Grayson*

When they say: Our tax dollars shouldn't go to pay for things like contraception.

You say: "To the people who are upset about their hard-earned tax money going to things they don't like: welcome to the fucking club. Reimburse me for the Iraq war and oil subsidies, and diaphragms are on me!" —*Jon Stewart*

How to Argue with Bible-Thumpers

When they say: There should be no separation of church and state.

You say: It's in the First Amendment, so too bad. Do we really want to go back to those wonderful Dark Ages when the church controlled everything? Let's consider for a second what George Carlin once said: "These two institutions screw us up enough on their own, so both of them together is certain death."

When they say: There is a war on Christianity.

You say: "Yes, the long war on Christianity. I pray that one day we may live in an America where Christians can worship freely! In broad daylight!

Openly wearing symbols of their religion…perhaps around their necks? And maybe—dare I dream it?—maybe one day there can be an openly Christian president. Or, perhaps, forty-three of them. Consecutively." —*Jon Stewart*

When they say: Jesus stood for conservative values.

You say: Jesus was a long-haired, sandal-wearing, peace-loving hippie who would have been much more at home at Burning Man than an NRA convention. He said it was easier for a camel to pass through the eye of a needle than for a rich man to get into heaven. And he healed the sick and fed the poor for free. Just like a good communist.

When they say: Homosexuality is wrong because the Bible says so.

You say: Allow me to cite a famous letter sent to Dr. Laura Schlessinger: "I would like to sell my daughter into slavery, as sanctioned in Exodus 21:7. In this day and age, what do you think would be a fair price for her?…I have a neighbor who insists on working on the Sabbath. Exodus 35:2. Am I morally obligated to kill him myself?…Most of my male friends get their hair trimmed, including the hair around their temples, even though this is expressly forbidden by Leviticus 19:27. How should they die?...I know from Leviticus 11:6-8 that touching the skin of a dead pig makes me unclean, but may I still play football if I wear gloves?"

When they say: Homosexuality is an affront to God.

You say: "How many gays must God create before we accept that he wants them around?" —*Minnesota state Rep. Steve Simon (D)*

When they say: We must do what Jesus would do.

You say: Except when it comes to, say, feeding the poor, caring for the needy, and turning the other cheek. That's just a lot of GOP talk, or as Stephen Colbert put it: "Mentioning Jesus in your speech: small government. Doing what Jesus asked: big government."

When they say: I believe that the universe is six thousand years old and that humans and dinosaurs coexisted.

You say: Actually you're thinking of *Land of the Lost.* You think they would have mentioned that in the Bible, or did I miss the part where Moses rides out of Egypt on a brontosaurus, or Adam and Eve are hanging out in Jurassic Park? Where was that? In the Book of T-Rex? And where does Tinker Bell figure into all this? No need to let science and facts get in the way of your fantasy history lesson.

When they say: In the name of Christianity, let's kill them all and let God sort them out.

You say: You keep using that word "Christianity." I don't think it means what you think it means.

When they say: We need to elect politicians who aren't afraid to talk about God.

You say: "I distrust politicians who talk about God, especially when it's the longest word they can spell." —*Andy Borowitz*

When they say: I trust my congressman/senator/president because he speaks directly to God every day.

You say: To paraphrase author Sam Harris, if someone said they were speaking to God through a hair dryer, everyone would think he was mad. I fail to see how the addition of a hair dryer makes it any more absurd.

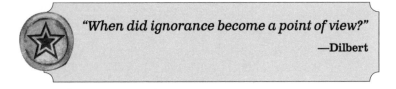

> *"When did ignorance become a point of view?"*
> —Dilbert

How to Rebut Other Conservative Drivel

When they say: The problem with America is teachers, public employees, Planned Parenthood, NPR, PBS, yada, yada, yada…

You say: "Remember when teachers, public employees, Planned Parenthood, NPR, and PBS crashed the stock market, wiped out half of our 401k's, took trillions in taxpayer-funded bailouts, spilled oil in the Gulf of Mexico, gave themselves billions in bonuses, and paid no taxes? Yeah, me neither."
—a status update that made the rounds on Facebook

When they say: Democrats act all high and mighty when they attack Republicans, but they've had plenty of their own scandals and are beholden to their own special interests.

You say: "We're not perfect, but they're nuts." *—Rep. Barney Frank (D-MA)*

When they say: Republicans believe government is the problem, not the solution.

You say: Call me crazy, but if Republicans don't believe in government, perhaps they shouldn't run for it.

When they say: The Republican Party is the pro-life party.

You say: Republicans are pro-life until you are actually born. To quote George Carlin: "[Conservatives] will do anything for the unborn. But once you're born, you're on your own. Pro-life conservatives are obsessed with the fetus from conception to nine months. After that, they don't want to know about you. They don't want to hear from you. No nothing. No neonatal care, no day care, no Head Start, no school lunch, no food stamps, no welfare, no nothing. If you're preborn, you're fine; if you're preschool, you're fucked."

When they say: Fox News is fair and balanced.

You say: Actually, according to Roger Ailes's original blueprint for Fox News found in the Nixon Library, the network was intended as a partisan ploy to circumvent the "prejudices of network news" and deliver right-wing propaganda to heartland television viewers. It's no wonder now that studies show Fox News viewers are typically the most misinformed of all news consumers. A better motto, as Jon Stewart suggested, would be: "Fox News: We Alter Reality. You Are Sold a Preconceived Narrative."

When they say: Liberalism is a scourge on society.

You say: Yeah, you're right. Curse you woman's suffrage and all you voting women! Curse you free black people who now have the same rights as everyone else! Curse you Social Security and Medicare for taking care of our elderly! Curse you Clean Air Act and Clean Water Act for making sure nobody pours garbage into my body! God bless all the conservatives who fought against this scourge, trying to keep America a dirtier, more oppressive country.

When they say: Liberals are elitists!

You say: What's more elitist than siding with wealthy interests and corporate greed-mongers over average working Americans? What's more elitist than saying that only you live in the "real America" and that everyone on the coasts is not a true American? And as Jon Stewart once put it, "What's more elite than believing that only you will go to heaven?"

When they say: We need a president who has business experience.

You say: "You really want to get into this argument with me? George Bush had business experience. There. I win." —*Bill Maher*

When they say: Mitt Romney looks like a president to me.

You say: I don't know what you look for in a president, but as Jon Stewart pointed out, Romney "looks like everyone who ever fired your dad." David Letterman thinks Romney "looks like that guy on the golf course in the Levitra commercial…He looks like the guy who goes to the restroom when the check comes…He looks like a guy who would run a seminar on condo flipping…He looks like he is the closer at a Cadillac dealership."

When they say: Mitt Romney is a man of principle.

You say: "Taking two positions on every issue, one on the left and one on the far right, doesn't make you a centrist; it makes you a charlatan." —*David Axelrod, adviser to President Obama*

When they say: Mitt Romney is a man of the people.

You say: This is a guy who helped lay off thousands

of American workers during his tenure at Bain Capital, while amassing obscene personal riches in the process. He owns multiple luxury homes, hides his money in the Cayman Islands, pays a tax rate of only 14% but thinks his taxes are too high so he proposes giving millionaires like himself another tax cut. Then he openly admits he doesn't care about the poor and enjoys firing people. He's not just the embodiment of the 1%. He's Mr. Burns with better hair. *Exxxxcellent!*

When they say: Rick Santorum is a man of principle.

You say: Here's a guy who says he wants government out of every aspect of people's lives, and yet he favor laws against contraception, sodomy, gay marriage, and abortions for victims of rape and incest. He says you're a snob if you think everyone should have the opportunity to go to college, and yet he has three degrees from three public universities. As Bill Maher put it, "Rick Santorum has come out against contraception and against college. He wants us literally to be fucking stupid."

When they say: We need more leaders in the mold of Newt Gingrich.

You say: We're talking about the same Newt Gingrich who was investigated by his own GOP majority for eighty-four ethics violations when he was House Speaker and was reprimanded in a 395–28 vote? The same Newt who shut down the government because Bill Clinton made him sit at the back of his plane? The same Newt who wants to repeal child labor laws, dismantle Social Security, and build a colony on the moon (presumably because his head can no longer be contained by Earth's atmosphere)? As Sam Donaldson said, "He has five ideas a day. One or two of them are brilliant, one or two of them are okay, and one of them is terrible—and he doesn't know the difference." Or, as columnist Peggy Noonan put it: "He is a human hand grenade who walks around with his hand on the pin, saying 'Watch this!'"

When they say: Sarah Palin is a great role model.

You say: There are so many ways to describe Palin: "Whack job," "Wasilla hillbilly," "Bible Spice," "Caribou Barbie," "quitter." Or as Bill Maher put it: "a vainglorious braggart, a liar, a whiner, a professional victim…a know-it-all, a chiseler, a bully who sells patriotism like a pimp, and the leader of a strange family of inbred weirdos straight out of *The Hills Have Eyes*." But role model is not one of them.

When they say: Michele Bachmann is not crazy.

You say: You're right; simply calling her crazy doesn't really do her justice. As *Rolling Stone*'s Matt Taibbi put it, Bachmann is the following: "a religious zealot whose brain is a raging electrical storm of divine visions and paranoid delusions," "one of the scariest sights in the entire American cultural tableau," "the T2 skeleton posing for a passport photo," and "grandiose crazy, late-stage Kim-Jong-Il crazy." Or, as Bill Maher put it more succinctly, "The floor of a cave called. It wants its bat shit back."

When they say: Jeb Bush would make a great president someday.

You say: "Bush presidencies are like *Caddyshack* movies. They should have stopped with one." —*David Letterman*

CHAPTER 7

The Conservative Hall of Shame

"I have only ever made one prayer to God, a very short one: 'Oh Lord, make my enemies ridiculous.' And God granted it."

—Voltaire

There is so much rampant hypocrisy and idiocy on the Right, it's nearly impossible to keep track of it all. But you can add extra bite to your arguments—and illustrate just how insane the other side is—by calling attention to the inglorious exploits of celebrated conservatives.

The late great political pundit Molly Ivins once said,

"The best way to get those bastards is to make people laugh at them." Fortunately, it's not hard, as you'll see from this rundown of some of the most prominent conservative morons, douche bags, and sex fiends who have disgraced national politics in recent years—and earned their place in the Conservative Hall of Shame.

The Wing of Batshit Crazy

MICHELE "CRAZY EYES" BACHMANN

Claim to shame: It wasn't enough to be known as the most batshit insane member of Congress. Michele Bachmann had to become the most batshit insane GOP presidential candidate, because no one puts crazy in the corner. In the informational black hole that constitutes her world, the Founding Fathers worked tirelessly to end slavery, the HPV vaccine causes mental retardation, gays and lesbians are "part of Satan," and God sends earthquakes and hurricanes when he gets upset about the "orgy" of government spending. If she's right about God's wrath, then she better get down in the storm cellar because— despite her staunch opposition to handouts and socialism of any kind—she took $250,000 in federal subsidies for her family's farm, $150,000 in government payments for her husband's "pray away the gay" therapy clinic, and aggressively pursued stimulus and EPA funds for her district. If hypocrisy could be measured in kilowatts, Bachmann could light up an entire amusement park.

SARAH PALIN, WINNER OF THE I-QUIT-AROD

Claim to shame: Once a rising star in the Republican Party, Sarah Palin was one of the nation's most popular governors and a celebrated GOP vice presidential candidate whom nearly 60 million Americans voted to put a heartbeat away from the nuclear launch codes. Then she turned into a griping sore loser, a famous quitter, a Facebook spammer, a nonsensical tweeter, a reality show star, and a crazy person riding a faux presidential campaign bus asking for money in a well-choreographed scam. No wonder she doesn't believe in evolution; she's living proof that Darwin was wrong. We'd devote more space to mocking this jabbering imbecile, but by the time this book is in print, she'll probably be reduced to spouting her latest "refudiations" on a megaphone to the few remaining moose she hasn't shot.

RICK "OOPS" PERRY

Claim to shame: Republicans were nearly orgasmic when Rick Perry tossed his Stetson into the 2012 presidential corral, quickly heralding him as the second coming of either George W. Bush or Jesus. Then he opened his mouth. The execution-happy governor accused the Fed chairman of treason, called Social Security a "Ponzi scheme," blamed gay soldiers for ruining Christmas, and was forced to explain why his family's hunting camp used to be known as "Niggerhead," among other missteps. It's hard (and a bit odd) to run for president of a country you would like your state to secede from, but it was made all the harder by his inept campaigning and disastrous debate performances. Perry will forever be remembered for his epic "oops" brain freeze, where he forgot the third federal agency he vowed to get rid of. (Although as David Letterman quipped, "It's nice to see a guy running for president who's only groping for words.") Humorist Andy Borowitz summed up Perry's candidacy best: "Rick Perry is qualified to be president in the same way that Olive Garden is qualified to be Italy."

GLENN "NAZI TOURETTE'S" BECK

Claim to shame: In an era of rampant right-wing paranoia, no one has done more to fan the flames of conspiratorial idiocy than Glenn Beck. After getting booted from his Fox News show, Beck now has more free time to spend with the voices in his head, when he's not rallying his disciples in Washington and Jerusalem and delivering his sermons on Mt. Crazy. He's been attempting to build his own Internet media empire, despite having lost most of his audience, which raises a question: When a blathering idiot falls in the forest, does he make a sound? Once described by Stephen King as "Satan's mentally challenged younger brother," Beck still sees himself as a modern-day Paul Revere who is convinced that the Obamanazis are plotting with Maoists to prevent people from worshipping Jesus, which, he will tell you, is exactly what the Nazis did to the Jews. As Jon Stewart noted, "The only real difference between Glenn Beck and Paul Revere is that when Paul Revere told you the British were coming, they were, in fact, coming."

ANN "COULTERGEIST"

Claim to shame: Nary a week goes by without this right-wing sociopath saying something ridiculous, racist, or insane. She has fantasized publicly about forcibly converting Muslims to Christianity; blowing up the New York Times building; making torture a televised spectator sport; and poisoning former Supreme Court Justice Stevens's crème brûlée. She believes nuclear radiation is good for you, that women should be stripped of the right to vote, and once boasted about Herman Cain by saying, "Our blacks are better than their blacks." Not even 9/11 widows have been spared her wrath, with Coulter saying, "I have never seen people enjoying their husband's death so much." As Keith Olbermann once said of her, "Honestly, if you were Ann Coulter's attorney at a sanity hearing, where could you possibly start?"

CHRISTINE "I'M NOT A WITCH" O'DONNELL

Claim to shame: No Tea Party candidate turned out to be nuttier, more unqualified, or hilariously entertaining than Delaware GOP Senate hopeful Christine O'Donnell. First, an old interview surfaced in which she boldly came out against masturbation, insisting that it was adultery (which Bill Maher found ironic because he said she owed her nomination to "a bunch of jack-offs"). Then, another interview was unearthed in which she talked about dabbling in witchcraft and having a date on a Satanic altar. After being widely ridiculed, O'Donnell felt compelled to run an ad in which she bizarrely declared, "I'm not a witch…I'm you." She lost the election by 20 percent. In a brief concession speech, she said, 'I'm melting,'" joked Craig Ferguson.

PAT ROBERTSON, CHARTER MEMBER, AMERICAN TALIBAN

Claim to shame: To recap some of his greatest hits, the good reverend and pillar of Christian love has prayed for the deaths of Supreme Court justices; suggested nuking the State Department; called for the assassination of foreign leaders; stated that the Haitian earthquake was a result of a pact with the devil; said it's OK for Christians to divorce spouses with Alzheimer's disease; and declared that gay people cause hurricanes. All of this from a guy who then advised the Republican candidates during the 2012 GOP primaries to tone down their crazy rhetoric, which is like George W. Bush telling you that war is not the answer.

SHARRON "OBTUSE" ANGLE

Claim to shame: Nevada Republicans picked the Milky Way of nutballs to run against Senate Democratic leader Harry Reid, and she did not disappoint with her laughable campaign. Angle openly requested that the media only ask her the questions she wanted to answer; told a group of Hispanic high school students that "some of you look a little more Asian to me"; and suggested that voters may need to consider a "Second Amendment remedy" to "take Harry Reid out." In other words, she's the total Tea Party package, so look for her to be the GOP's 2016 presidential nominee.

JAN "HEADLESS CORPSES" BREWER

Claim to shame: With her state facing a multitude of problems, Arizona Gov. Jan Brewer did what your typical conservative xenophobe would do: blame the Mexicans. Brewer signed a draconian law that allowed police to check the immigration status of people who they "thought" might be illegal, and defended it by falsely claiming border violence had gotten so bad that there had been beheadings in the Arizona desert. Despite the torrent of negative publicity and boycotts she prompted, Arizonans still re-elected her by a large margin, because that's what right-wingers do when they're holding the batshit cards; they double down.

> *"Two things are infinite—the universe and human stupidity, and I'm not sure about the universe."*
>
> —Albert Einstein

The Wing of Douche Bags

MITT "FLIP FLOP" ROMNEY

Claim to shame: The former Massachusetts governor-turned-Republican-presidential candidate has flip-flopped on so many issues, he makes Brett Favre look like Mr. Decisive. He was for Romneycare in Massachusetts before he was against it (now known as "Obamacare"). He was pro-choice before he became pro-life. He believed in man-made global warming before he became a denier. Luckily, there are a couple of things Romney has always been unflinchingly in favor of: strapping dogs to the roof of his car on long family road trips, because that's how he treats man's best friend; and playing chauffeur to corporate fat cats, because, in his own words, "corporations are people too," and you better believe they get to ride *in* the car.

DONALD "YOU'RE FIRED" TRUMP

Claim to shame: Where to start? The dead rodent on his head? *The Apprentice?* The four wives? Taking up the birther cause and insisting Obama wasn't born in America (even after he released his long-form birth certificate)? Trump teased a GOP presidential run and enjoyed an initial love-fest with the Right, before the hot air ran out of the bag and Trump pulled the plug on what turned out to be just another publicity stunt. The decision, Conan O'Brien joked, came as "devastating news for Trump's supporters—all of whom are late night comedians."

RUPERT MURDOCH, A.K.A. MR. BURNS

Claim to shame: Propagandist, phone hacker, war monger, right-wing apologist, tax evader, union buster, oil imperialist, defender of repressive regimes—and those are Rupert Murdoch's good qualities. The Australian-born billionaire who heads Fox News's parent company, News Corp., is a one-man wrecking crew on the truth, having journalistic principles that make the *National Enquirer* look respectable. Shame fell on his media empire amid revelations that reporters for his *News of the World* publication had hacked into the phones of British celebrities, government officials, and victims of high-profile crimes and terrorist attacks. When Murdoch and his equally vile son were brought to testify before the British parliament, they did exactly what you'd expect someone of their integrity to do: they blamed others.

THE KOCH BROTHERS,
GOP CORPORATE OVERLORDS

Claim to shame: Über-wealthy conservative puppet masters David and Charles Koch earned their fortune the old-fashioned way, by inheriting it, and now use their powers for evil. Owners of Koch Industries, the Koch brothers have been one of the main funders behind the Tea Party and other nefarious right-wing activities, like Wisconsin's anti-union campaign. Investigations have also shown that they've been behind such amazingly un-American activities as illegally selling chemical equipment to Iran, stealing oil from federal land, and lying to regulators about toxic emissions. Even the brother of these nimrods, William, who dropped out of the family business, called the company an "organized crime" operation. Yet Republicans from every state will line up at their door to grovel at their feet and ask for campaign contributions, a practice known throughout political circles as "sucking Koch."

SCOTT "IMPERIAL" WALKER

Claim to shame: In the fierce competition for worst Republican governor in America, Wisconsin Gov. Scott Walker is in a douche class all by himself. Upon taking office, he created a deficit crisis so he could push through a union-busting bill that stripped public workers of their collective bargaining rights—because in these tough economic times, who better to stick it to than those "fat cat" teachers, nurses, and sanitation workers? The real goal of all these efforts, of course, is to break unions so as to deprive Democrats of some of their biggest campaign contributors. Walker became a huge conservative hero, and despite attempts to try to recall him, he could one day get the Republican nomination for president because, as Bill Maher noted, "He has that special quality that every member of the Republican base can relate to—he's a huge asshole."

RICK "PLEASE DON'T GOOGLE MY LAST NAME" SANTORUM

Claim to shame: Best known for his sanctimonious moralizing and unapologetic gay bashing, Republican presidential candidate Rick Santorum will forever be remembered for the infamous interview he gave comparing homosexuality to bestiality and pedophilia. He said the definition of marriage has never included "man on child, man on dog, or whatever the case may be" (to which the reporter replied, "I'm sorry, I didn't think I was going to talk about 'man on dog' with a United States senator; it's sort of freaking me out"). Santorum's critics lashed back with a Google bombing campaign to associate Santorum's surname with a sexual act—specifically "the frothy mixture of lube and fecal matter that is sometimes the byproduct of anal sex," which remained the number-one Google search result for "Santorum" throughout his failed 2012 presidential run. Despite being taunted by headlines such as "Santorum surges," "runs hard," and "comes from behind" on his way to losing to Mitt Romney, Santorum vowed to rebuild America from "the bottom up." Or, as Jon Stewart said mockingly, "Mitt Romney may have come out on top of us, but we will stay in and not heed the calls to pull out. Fueled by your spunk, it's on to Super Tuesday, where we will toss that man's salad from Ohio to Tennessee."

GEORGE "THEY MISUNDERESTIMATED ME" W. BUSH

Claim to shame: To recap the nightmarish Bush years: he stole an election, ignored intelligence warnings before 9/11, botched the Afghanistan war, lied us into the Iraq war quagmire, alienated our allies, let the city of New Orleans drown, blew the surplus, and led us to the brink of economic collapse. Where Bush goes, disaster has always followed. Just look at the Texas Rangers. As Bill Maher once put it, "Maybe you're just not lucky. I'm not saying you don't love this country; I'm just wondering how much worse it could be if you were on the other side. So yes, God does speak to you, and what he's saying is, 'Take a hint.'"

DICK "DARTH VADER" CHENEY

Claim to shame: Blew up the planet Alderaan with the Death Star, killed all the Jedi except Yoda, slaughtered all the younglings in cold blood, and once choked a guy with the Force. And what did Cheney have to say for himself? "I was honored to be compared to Darth Vader," he told talk show host Laura Ingraham in 2011 while hawking his memoir.

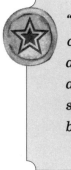

"Every week there's a new gay Republican outed. I have a feeling that 'big tent' they're always talking about is in their pants. There are so many Republicans in the closet, their symbol shouldn't be an elephant; it should be a moth."

—Bill Maher

The Wing of Sex Fiends, Perverts, and Adulterers

NEWT "I'M SO COMMITTED TO MARRIAGE, I CAN'T STOP DOING IT" GINGRICH

Claim to shame: The former House Speaker and GOP presidential candidate married his high school geometry teacher a year after graduating. Years later, he declared she wasn't "young enough or pretty enough to be the wife of the president" and showed up at the hospital while she was undergoing cancer treatment to discuss the terms of their divorce. He asked his second wife for a divorce after she was diagnosed with multiple sclerosis by phoning her on Mother's Day, in the midst of carrying on an affair with a congressional staffer twenty-three years his junior—all while decrying Bill Clinton's moral failings and orchestrating his impeachment. When later running for president, he explained that it was his love for his country that made him cheat on his wives. "Apparently he misunderstood the phrase, 'Please rise for the Pledge of Allegiance,'" joked Conan O'Brien.

HERMAN "SUGAR" CAIN

Claim to shame: When it was discovered that the Godfather of pizza had baked his salami in too many different ovens,

Cain's once surging presidential campaign came to a sadly predictable end. While the stream of sexual harassment charges was certainly damaging, and the exposure of a long-term extramarital affair embarrassing, it was his alleged mistresses' description of mundane sex that voters couldn't tolerate. ("One time we were having sex, and I was looking up at the ceiling, thinking about, 'What am I going to buy at the grocery store tomorrow?'") In suspending his campaign, Cain once again regurgitated a quote that he had earlier attributed to a poet but was later discovered to be from the Donna Summer song "The Power of One" in *Pokemon: The Movie 2000*, when he said, "Life can be a challenge. Life can seem impossible. It's never easy when there is so much on the line. But you and I can make a difference." Perhaps Cain meant to quote one of Summer's other songs: "I need some hot stuff baby this evenin'. I need some hot stuff baby, tonight. Gotta have some lovin' tonight." Lamenting the end of his campaign, Stephen Colbert put it best: "That is a shame. He touched so many people."

ARNOLD SCHWARZENEGGER, THE SPERMINATOR

Claim to shame: Arnold Schwarzenegger's groping and womanizing exploits were well known when Californians elected him governor back in 2003. But what they didn't know when he took the oath of office was that "the Sperminator" had already gone "Jingle All the Way" with the family maid and produced a love child—or as Craig Ferguson referred to it, an "it's-OK-Maria's-asleep child." He eventually came clean (that's what she said) after leaving office, and his wife, Maria Shriver, promptly left him. But as Bill Maher joked, "Nobody believes Arnold could have kept this from Maria Shriver for ten years because that would have required acting."

MARK "HIKING THE APPALACHIAN TRAIL" SANFORD

Claim to shame: After he went missing for several days, South Carolina Gov. Mark Sanford became a national laughingstock when it turned out he was not "hiking the Appalachian Trail," as his staff claimed, but was in fact off in Argentina chasing tail. "It turned out he was down there because he was sleeping with a woman from Argentina. Once again, foreigners taking jobs that Americans won't do," David Letterman joked. "Just another politician with a conservative mind and a liberal penis," quipped Jon Stewart.

LARRY "WIDE STANCE" CRAIG

Claim to shame: When he wasn't busy crusading against homosexuals, ex-Sen. Larry Craig (R-estroom) was doing what most outspoken "family values" Republicans do: prowling for gay hookers. Craig gave new meaning to the word "caucusing" when he was caught playing footsie in an airport men's room with his infamous "wide stance." Needless to say, the comedians had a field day mocking Craig, or as David Letterman dubbed him, "The Restroom Don Juan." Craig announced his resignation, then reversed his decision after "talking it over with guy in stall number three" (Conan O'Brien), angering his Republican colleagues, some of whom "stopped having sex with him" (Jimmy Kimmel). The staunchly anti-gay lawmaker denied being a hypocrite, saying, "Hey, I wasn't trying to marry the cop in the bathroom" (Conan). Later, he was inducted into the Idaho Hall of Fame—not the entire hall, "just the men's room" (Jay Leno).

JOHN "I'LL TAKE YOUR WIFE, PLEASE" ENSIGN

Claim to shame: It's one thing when a married Republican senator bangs a staff member (or as it's known on Capitol Hill, Tuesday). But it's quite another when that staff member is the wife of your best friend and chief of staff. Such was the case with Sen. John Ensign (R-NV), a family values moralizer and former champion of Bill Clinton's impeachment, whose sordid affair was a subject of ongoing discussion in his congressional prayer group, known as C Street. When the spurned spouses found out, Ensign fired his mistress and his chief of staff, and had his rich parents pay them just under $100,000 in hush money. He eventually resigned in 2011, amid an ethics inquiry, but insisted that he had not violated "any law, rule, or standard of conduct of the Senate," which unfortunately might be the only truth this low-life ever uttered.

BILL O'REILLY, FALAFEL FETISHIST

Claim to shame: The Fox News bloviator settled a sexual harassment lawsuit brought by a former producer who accused him of talking to her in explicit terms about "phone sex, vibrators, threesomes, masturbation, the loss of his virginity, and sexual fantasies." In the most notorious sexual scenario, O'Reilly confused a loofah for a falafel, attempting to seduce his victim by describing lewd acts he hoped to perform on her in the shower using deep-fried chickpeas. Around the same time, he wrote in *The O'Reilly Factor for Kids*, "And guys, if you exploit a girl, it will come back to get you. That's called 'karma.'"

SENATOR DAVID "D.C. MADAM" VITTER

Claim to shame: In his first term as Republican senator from Louisiana, Vitter admitted to frequenting prostitutes after *Hustler* magazine identified his phone number on the infamous "D.C. Madam's" client list. Vitter explained it away by saying he had already "asked for and received forgiveness from God," but more important, he received forgiveness from his wife, who once said she would pull a Lorena Bobbitt if her husband ever cheated on her. Despite the scandal, Louisiana voters overwhelmingly re-elected Vitter to a second term, presumably because this is the kind of behavior they've come to expect from the party's most stalwart family values defenders.

RUDY GIULIANI, AMERICA'S ADULTERER

Claim to shame: After carrying on an affair while serving as New York mayor, Giuliani announced at a 2000 press conference that he was divorcing his second wife—without bothering to tell her first. Because if you're going to leave the mother of your two children, who better to deliver the news delicately than New York tabloid reporters? Later it was revealed that while Giuliani was carrying on his affair, he billed taxpayers for security expenses incurred during his love romps in the Hamptons; attempted to hide those expenses by billing obscure city agencies; and enlisted the NYPD to serve as a personal taxi service to chauffeur around his mistress on long trips and walk her dog.

REVEREND TED "SAY NO TO GAY MARRIAGE, SAY YES TO GAY HOOKERS" HAGGARD

Claim to shame: A one-time spiritual adviser to President Bush, Haggard resigned as president of the thirty-million-member National Association of Evangelicals amid allegations he had been having methamphetamine-fueled gay sex. The hooker he frequented over a period of three years said he decided to out Haggard because of his hypocritical moralizing and outspoken opposition to gay marriage. "You know you're in trouble when you've ceded the moral high ground to a drug-dealing prostitute," quipped Jon Stewart.

MARK "I'M NEVER TOO BUSY TO SPANK IT" FOLEY

Claim to shame: Rep. Mark Foley (R-Fla.), former chairman of the House Caucus on Missing and Exploited Children, was forced to resign in 2006 amid revelations that he had engaged in sexually explicit IM chats with underage male pages. Some excerpts: "How's my favorite young stud doing?...Did you spank it this weekend?...Strip down and get relaxed...Good, so you're getting horny?...Cute butt bouncing in the air... Get a ruler and measure it for me...(Page: 'My mom is yelling')...Cool, I hope she didn't see anything." As Jon Stewart noted, Foley "spent most of his career protecting children from Internet stalkers. Turns out he was doing it so he could have them all to himself."

STROM THURMOND, PUTTING THE "DIX" IN "DIXIECRAT"

Claim to shame: An eight-term senator and onetime presidential candidate, Thurmond was a staunch advocate of segregation, despite having fathered an illegitimate daughter at age twenty-two after a tryst with a sixteen-year-old African American girl working as the family maid (which wasn't revealed until after his death at age one hundred). As Jon Stewart joked, "Thurmond devoted much of his life to the cause of racial segregation, but when it came to separating whites and blacks, he did make an exception for his penis."

"The tyrant fears laughter more than the assassin's bullet."

—Robert A. Heinlein

★ **CHAPTER 8** ★

How to Use Conservatives' Own Words against Them

"Voters quickly forget what a man says."

—**President Richard Nixon**

One of the best ways to hammer away at conservatives is to smear them with their own words. Here are some handy quotes to keep in your arsenal that you can throw at your opponents when you need examples of right-wing idiocy, derangement, mendacity, incompetence, or sociopathy. Fortunately, there's an almost limitless supply.

Stunningly Moronic Conservative Quotes

"I'm not concerned about the very poor. We have a safety net there."

—Republican presidential candidate Mitt Romney

"I like being able to fire people who provide services to me."

—Mitt Romney, while advocating for consumer choice in health insurance plans

"I know what it's like to worry about whether or not you are going to get fired. … There are times when I wondered whether I was going to get a pink slip."

—Mitt Romney, attempting to identify with the problems of average folk

"I'll tell you what, ten-thousand bucks? $10,000 bet?"

—Mitt Romney, attempting to make a wager with Rick Perry during a Republican presidential debate

"I have some great friends who are NASCAR team owners."

—Mitt Romney

"I should tell my story. I'm also unemployed."

—Mitt Romney, speaking to unemployed people in Florida. (Romney's net worth is over $200 million)

"Ann drives a couple of Cadillacs."

—Mitt Romney, referring to his wife

"I don't even consider myself wealthy."

—Ann Romney

"Well, I think you hit a reset button for the fall campaign. Everything changes. It's almost like an Etch-a-Sketch. You can kind of shake it up, and we start all over again."

—Mitt Romney adviser Eric Fehrnstrom, comparing Romney's presidential campaign to an erasable toy and suggesting that he could easily reinvent the hard-right positions he took during the Republican primaries

"He who warned, uh, the British that they weren't gonna be takin' away our arms, uh, by ringing those bells, and um, makin' sure as he's riding his horse through town to send those warning shots and bells that we were going to be sure and we were going to be free, and we were going to be armed."

—former Republican vice presidential candidate Sarah Palin, botching the history of Paul Revere's midnight ride

"But we also know that the very founders that wrote those documents worked tirelessly until slavery was no more in the United States. And I think it is high time that we recognize the contribution of our forbearers who worked tirelessly—men like John Quincy Adams, who would not rest until slavery was extinguished in the country."

—Rep. Michele Bachmann (R-MN), speaking at an Iowan's for Tax Relief event in January 2011.

The Founding Fathers did not work "tirelessly" to end slavery and in fact enshrined it in the Constitution. Moreover, John Quincy Adams, who was eight when the Declaration of Independence was signed, was not one of the Founding Fathers.

"It's like a derivative of actual pepper. It's a food product, essentially."

—Fox News anchor Megyn Kelly, downplaying the physical effects of pepper spray on student Occupy protesters at UC Davis

"We don't know what those other [climate change] cycles were caused by in the past. It could be dinosaur flatulence. Who knows?"

—Rep. Dana Rohrabacher (R-CA), during a
congressional hearing on global warming

"There is a growing body of evidence that radiation in excess of what the government says is actually good for you and actually reduces cancer."

—Ann Coulter, arguing that the 2011
Japanese nuclear crisis was overblown
and that people should not be concerned
about the radioactive plume

"Halloween is a liberal holiday because we're teaching our children to beg for something for free…We're teaching kids to knock on other people's doors and ask for a handout."

—Fox News host Sean Hannity

"I believe in an America where millions of Americans believe in an America that's the America millions of Americans believe in. That's the America I love."

—Mitt Romney

"We used to hustle over the border for health care we received in Canada. And I think now, isn't that ironic?"

—Sarah Palin, admitting that her family used to get treatment in Canada's single-payer health-care system, despite having demonized such government-run programs as socialized medicine that will lead to death-panel-like rationing

"If Barack Obama begins taxing me more than 50 percent, which is very possible, I don't know how much longer I'm going to do this. I like my job, but there comes a point when taxation becomes oppressive."

—Fox News host Bill O'Reilly, threatening to quit if President Obama raised taxes on millionaires

"I will tell you: It's three agencies of government, when I get there, that are gone: Commerce, Education, and the—what's the third one there? Let's see…OK. So Commerce, Education, and the…The third agency of government I would—I would do away with the Education, the… Commerce and—let's see—I can't. The third one, I can't. Sorry. Oops."

—Republican presidential candidate
Rick Perry, forgetting his plan to
abolish the Department of Energy in
an epic brain freeze during a GOP debate

"By the time I feed my family, I have maybe $400,000 left over."

—Rep. John Fleming (R-LA),
crying poverty over the prospect
of increasing taxes on the wealthy

"We needed to have the press be our friend… We wanted them to ask the questions we want to answer so that they report the news the way we want it to be reported."

—failed Nevada GOP Senate candidate
Sharron Angle, during a Fox News interview

"President Obama wants everybody in America to go to college. What a snob ... Oh, I understand why he wants you to go to college. He wants to remake you in his image."

—Rick Santorum, campaigning for president while speaking to a Tea Party group

"Well, what I want them to know is just like, John Wayne was from Waterloo, Iowa. That's the kind of spirit that I have, too."

—Rep. Michele Bachmann, getting her John Waynes mixed up during an interview after launching her presidential campaign in Waterloo, Iowa, where she grew up. The beloved movie star John Wayne was born in Winterset, Iowa, three hours away. The John Wayne who hailed from Waterloo was John Wayne Gacy, a notorious serial killer.

"I'll tell you why [religion is] not a scam, in my opinion. Tide goes in, tide goes out. Never a miscommunication. You can't explain that. You can't explain why the tide goes in."

—Fox News host Bill O'Reilly, attempting to prove the existence of God

"It is not enough to be abstinent with other people; you also have to be abstinent alone. The Bible says that lust in your heart is committing adultery. You can't masturbate without lust!... You're going to be pleasing each other. And if he already knows what pleases him and he can please himself, then why am I in the picture?"

—failed Delaware GOP Senate candidate
Christine O'Donnell, advocating against
masturbation in a 1996 MTV interview

"PETA is not happy that my dog likes fresh air."

—Republican presidential candidate
Mitt Romney in 2007, responding to criticism
from People for the Ethical Treatment of
Animals following revelations that he had
once put the family dog in a carrier and strapped it
to the roof of his car during a 12-hour road trip

"I won't place one more dollar of debt upon the backs of my kids and grandkids unless we structurally reform the way this town spends money!"

—Rep. Joe Walsh (R-IL), a tax-bashing Tea Party champion, lecturing President Obama about fiscal responsibility in an online video, despite facing allegations that he himself owed $117,437 in child support to his ex-wife and three children at the time. Walsh claimed he failed to make the payments because he "had no money," even though he loaned his own campaign $35,000. Later, the right-wing Family Research Council honored Walsh with an award for his "unwavering support of the family."

"'Refudiate,' 'misunderestimate,' 'wee-wee'd up.' English is a living language. Shakespeare liked to coin new words too. Got to celebrate it!"

—a tweet sent by Sarah Palin in response to being ridiculed for inventing the word "refudiate," proudly mistaking her illiteracy for literary genius

"Well, you know, that's the problem in America: we're always having elections."

—Sen. John Cornyn (R-TX)

Breathtakingly Delusional Conservative Quotes

"Corporations are people, my friend...of course they are. Everything corporations earn ultimately goes to the people. Where do you think it goes? Whose pockets? Whose pockets? People's pockets. Human beings, my friend."

—Republican presidential candidate
Mitt Romney to a heckler at the
Iowa State Fair who suggested that
taxes should be raised on corporations
as part of balancing the budget

"I don't think we came from monkeys. I think that's ridiculous. I haven't seen a half monkey/ half person yet."

—Glenn Beck, on evolution

"Texas is a unique place. When we came in the union in 1845, one of the issues was that we would be able to leave if we decided to do that. You know, my hope is that America, and Washington in particular, pays attention. We've got a great union. There is absolutely no reason to dissolve it. But if Washington continues to thumb their nose at the American people, you know, who knows what may come out of that?"

—Texas Gov. and Republican presidential candidate Rick Perry, speaking to a reporter after he spoke at a Tea Party rally outside Austin's city hall

"Capital punishment is our society's recognition of the sanctity of human life."

—Sen. Orrin Hatch (R-UT), speaking on the Senate floor about his support for the death penalty

"Exercise freaks…are the ones putting stress on the health-care system."

—Rush Limbaugh

"One of the things I will talk about, that no president has talked about before, is I think the dangers of contraception in this country...Many of the Christian faith have said, well, that's okay, contraception is okay. It's not okay. It's a license to do things in a sexual realm that is counter to how things are supposed to be."

—ex-Sen. Rick Santorum (R-PA)

"Al Gore's not going to be rounding up Jews and exterminating them. It is the same tactic, however. The goal is different. The goal is globalization... And you must silence all dissenting voices. That's what Hitler did. That's what Al Gore, the U.N., and everybody on the global warming bandwagon [are doing]."

—Glenn Beck on his radio program

"I wish the American media would take a great look at the views of the people in Congress and find out: are they pro-America or anti-America?"

—Rep. Michelle Bachmann (R-MN),
calling for a new McCarthyism

"What does it say about the college coed Sandra Fluke who goes before a congressional committee and essentially says that she must be paid to have sex—what does that make her? It makes her a slut, right? It makes her a prostitute. She wants to be paid to have sex. She's having so much sex she can't afford the contraception. She wants you and me and the taxpayers to pay her to have sex."

—Rush Limbaugh, referring to a Georgetown Law School student who was denied the right to speak at a congressional hearing on contraception, where she planned to discuss a friend of hers who needed contraception to prevent the growth of cysts. After Limbaugh's remark sparked controversy, he doubled down, saying, "So Miss Fluke and the rest of you feminazis, here's the deal. If we are going to pay for your contraceptives and thus pay for you to have sex, we want something. We want you to post the videos online so we can all watch."

"Now, how can I be anti-woman? I even judged the Miss America pageant."

—Rush Limbaugh

"I find it hard to disagree with Rush Limbaugh on topics."

—Mitt Romney in 2010

"What am I going to do for Earth Day? I'm going to have every one of my cars driven as much as possible today; I've got my airplane flying to Los Angeles and back; let's see, all the lights are going to be on, the air conditioning down to 68 degrees in all, well, four out of the five houses. The property manager likes it at 65. Let's see, we're going to have all kinds of beef. I'm fixing Allen Brothers all weekend long. I personally am going to see to it that we lose two acres of rainforest."

—Rush Limbaugh

"Sometimes dictators have good ideas."

—failed Nevada GOP Senate candidate Sharron Angle, referring to former Chilean dictator Augusto Pinochet and privatizing Social Security, in remarks at a private meet-and-greet in the 2010 campaign season, as reported by the *Las Vegas Sun*

"Hunger can be a positive motivator."

> —former State Rep. Cynthia Davis
> (R-Missouri), arguing in a press release
> against a program that feeds poor children,
> suggesting they should get jobs instead

"My grandmother was not a highly educated woman, but she told me as a small child to quit feeding stray animals. You know why? Because they breed. You're facilitating the problem if you give an animal or a person ample food supply. They will reproduce, especially ones that don't think too much further than that. And so what you've got to do is you've got to curtail that type of behavior. They don't know any better."

> —South Carolina Lt. Gov. Andre Bauer,
> arguing that government food assistance
> to lower-income residents, including
> food stamps or free school lunches,
> encourages a culture of dependence

"It is tragic what we do in the poorest neighborhoods, entrapping children in child laws which are truly stupid...These schools should get rid of unionized janitors, have one master janitor, pay local students to take care of the school."

—Republican presidential candidate Newt Gingrich, calling for an end to child labor laws

"If we took away women's right to vote, we'd never have to worry about another Democrat president. It's kind of a pipe dream, it's a personal fantasy of mine, but I don't think it's going to happen. And it is a good way of making the point that women are voting so stupidly, at least single women."

—Ann Coulter

"The feminist agenda is not about equal rights for women. It is about a socialist, anti-family political movement that encourages women to leave their husbands, kill their children, practice witchcraft, destroy capitalism, and become lesbians.'"

—Rev. Pat Robertson, Christian televangelist and former Republican presidential candidate

"I think that two wrongs don't make a right. And I have been in the situation of counseling young girls, not 13, but 15, who have had very at-risk, difficult pregnancies. And my counsel was to look for some alternatives, which they did. And they found that they had made what was really a lemon situation into lemonade."

—failed Nevada GOP Senate nominee and Tea Party favorite Sharron Angle, explaining why she is against abortion even in cases of rape or incest

"Freedom is about authority. Freedom is about the willingness of every single human being to cede to lawful authority a great deal of discretion about what you do."

—former New York Mayor Rudy Giuliani

"When I see a 9/11 victim family on television, or whatever, I'm just like, 'Oh shut up.' I'm so sick of them because they're always complaining."

—Glenn Beck in 2005

"I don't know how much God has to do to get the attention of the politicians. We've had an earthquake; we've had a hurricane. He said, 'Are you going to start listening to me here?' Listen to the American people because the American people are roaring right now. They know government is on a morbid obesity diet and we've got to rein in the spending."

—Republican presidential candidate Michele Bachmann, suggesting at a campaign event in Florida that the 2011 East Coast earthquake and hurricane were messages from God

"[Liberal rhetoric] now is so over the top, it's so vicious, it's so mean, it's so cruel, and I don't hear this coming from conservatives about liberals."

—Fox News host Sean Hannity, with a straight face. After playing that video clip on his show, Jon Stewart quipped, "You don't? That is, if I may say, some of the most free-range, organically grown disingenuous, ideologically marinated, un-self-awareness I've ever seen in the wild."

"I have been nervous about this interview with you because what I feel like saying is, 'Sir, prove to me that you are not working with our enemies'… And I know you're not. I'm not accusing you of being an enemy, but that's the way I feel, and I think a lot of Americans will feel that way."

—Glenn Beck, interviewing Rep. Keith Ellison (D-MN), the first Muslim U.S. congressman

"Literally, if we took away the minimum wage—if conceivably it was gone—we could potentially virtually wipe out unemployment completely because we would be able to offer jobs at whatever level."

—Rep. Michelle Bachmann (R-MN)

"We can't be lulled into complacency. You have to remember that Adolf Hitler was elected in a democratic Germany. I'm not comparing him to Adolf Hitler. What I'm saying is there is the potential."

—Rep. Paul Broun (R-GA), expressing fears one week after Barack Obama was elected president in 2008 that he would create a security force akin to the Gestapo to impose a Marxist dictatorship

"This president I think has exposed himself over and over again as a guy who has a deep-seated hatred for white people or the white culture...I'm not saying he doesn't like white people; I'm saying he has a problem. This guy is, I believe, a racist."

—Glenn Beck on Fox News Channel

Shockingly Sociopathic Conservative Quotes

"The only way to reduce the number of nuclear weapons is to use them."

—Rush Limbaugh

"It's going to be twenty feet high. It's going to have barbed wire on the top. It's going to be electrified. And there's going to be a sign on the other side saying, 'It will kill you—Warning.'"

—failed GOP presidential candidate Herman Cain, on his plan to secure the border, which he later said was a "joke"

"We need somebody to put rat poisoning in Justice Stevens's crème brûlée. That's just a joke, for you in the media."

> —Ann Coulter, on how to create
> a vacancy in the Supreme Court

"I just wish [Hurricane] Katrina had only hit the United Nations building, nothing else, just had flooded them out, and I wouldn't have rescued them."

> —Bill O'Reilly, on his radio show

"I hope that's not where we're going, but you know if this Congress keeps going the way it is, people are really looking toward those Second Amendment remedies and saying my goodness what can we do to turn this country around? I'll tell you the first thing we need to do is take Harry Reid out."

> —failed Nevada GOP Senate candidate
> and Tea Party favorite Sharron Angle, floating
> the possibility of armed insurrection during an
> interview with a right-wing talk-show host

"I'm thinking about killing Michael Moore, and I'm wondering if I could kill him myself, or if I would need to hire somebody to do it...No, I think I could. I think he could be looking me in the eye, you know, and I could just be choking the life out. Is this wrong? I stopped wearing my What Would Jesus—band—Do, and I've lost all sense of right and wrong now. I used to be able to say, 'Yeah, I'd kill Michael Moore,' and then I'd see the little band: What Would Jesus Do? And then I'd realize, 'Oh, you wouldn't kill Michael Moore. Or at least you wouldn't choke him to death.' And you know, well, I'm not sure."

—Glenn Beck in 2005, responding to the question
"What would people do for $50 million?"

"If Al Qaeda comes in here and blows you up, we're not going to do anything about it. We're going to say, look, every other place in America is off limits to you, except San Francisco. You want to blow up the Coit Tower? Go ahead."

—Fox News host Bill O'Reilly in 2005,
after San Francisco voted to ban
military recruiters from city schools

"If I were to lose my mind right now and pick up one of you and dash your head against the floor and kill you, would that be right?"

—Alan Keyes, 2000 GOP presidential candidate, speaking to a class of fifth graders about abortion during a campaign appearance in New Hampshire

"I admired Hitler, for instance, because he came from being a little man with almost no formal education, up to power. I admire him for being such a good public speaker and for what he did with it."

—Arnold Schwarzenegger, explaining who his heroes were during a 1975 interview during the filming of a documentary, *Pumping Iron*.

"It's just a good thing I can't pack a gun on the Senate floor."

—Sen. Tom Coburn (R-OK), expressing frustration over how his colleagues have handled the economy, calling them "a class of career elitists" and "cowards"

For more ridiculous right-wing quotes, check out the companion calendar to this book, "365 Wrongs from the Right," by Daniel Kurtzman (www.wrongsfromtheright.com).

After-*words*

"If you can't answer a man's argument, all is not lost; you can still call him vile names."

—Elbert Hubbard

When All Else Fails: 125,000 Ways to Insult Conservatives

Can't persuade anyone to your way of thinking? Kill 'em with words instead. The following handy chart contains 125,000 potential insults that you can lob at conservatives.

Choose a word from each column, string them together, and fire away at all the "unmedicated, Fox News-parroting assclowns" or "brainwashed, fact-loathing whack jobs" in your midst. Think of it as your very own Magic Hate Ball.

Column A	Column B	Column C
unhinged	Bible-thumping	wingnuts
unmedicated	gas-guzzling	extremists
brainless	gun-fondling	blowhards
slack-jawed	knuckle-dragging	rednecks
inbred	Constitution-trampling	hypocrites
puritanical	Fox News-parroting	hatriots
delusional	race-baiting	crackpots
impotent	Kool-Aid-drinking	douche bags
depraved	fact-loathing	one-percenters
intolerant	reality-denying	morons
psychotic	NRA-worshipping	losers
uninformed	trailer-dwelling	sociopaths
deranged	mullet-wearing	whack jobs
bitter	tobacco-juice-dribbling	weasels
clueless	torture-cheering	imbeciles
greedy	Ponzi-scheming	halfwits
shameless	stock-manipulating	Neanderthals
heartless	health care-denying	Rethuglicans
arrogant	pitchfork-wielding	lunatics
obnoxious	planet-trampling	yahoos
brain-dead	conspiracy-theorizing	hicks

Column A	Column B	Column C
ignorant	waterboard-loving	nutbars
mindless	Civil War-reenacting	zealots
paranoid	Christianity-bastardizing	xenophobes
repressed	book-burning	nut jobs
maniacal	glacier-hating	secessionists
illiterate	Hummer-loving	brownshirts
witless	Scripture-spouting	lemmings
irrational	cave-dwelling	yokels
unstable	pollution-spewing	fascists
crazy	Rapture-lusting	misanthropes
brainwashed	execution-cheering	hotheads
uneducated	corporate-crime-forgiving	trolls
insane	ammo-stockpiling	teatards
rabid	Confederate flag-waving	whacktivists
sniveling	air-fouling	assclowns
gap-toothed	Earth-defiling	idiots
home-schooled	Viagra-depending	patrio-fascists
fundamentalist	God-misappropriating	hypochristians
sanctimonious	class-warfare-waging	hatemongers
primitive	Wall Street-worshipping	bed wetters
soulless	Social Security-privatizing	bottom-feeders

Column A	**Column B**	**Column C**
lobotomized	war-drumming	mouth-breathers
drooling	corporate-whoring	ignoramuses
blathering	history-revising	homophobes
buffoonish	homeless-kicking	fearmongers
incoherent	doomsday-preaching	propagandists
fanatical	bunker-dwelling	McCarthyites
selfish	roadkill-eating	evangeliclowns
reactionary	baby-seal-clubbing	neocon-artists

Acknowledgments

This book would not have been necessary if it hadn't been for the politicians on both sides who have worked so diligently to divide the country. Nor would it have been possible—or at least not as much fun to write—without the inspiration provided by comedians like Jon Stewart, Stephen Colbert, and Bill Maher, who put politics in perspective and help dull the pain.

I am indebted to my editor, Shana Drehs, and to Deb Werksman, Sean Murray, and the staff at Sourcebooks, whose hard work and enthusiasm made this book a reality, and to Barret Neville, whose editorial guidance and vision helped shape this project.

Many thanks to Thomas Fahy, who offered indispensable feedback, careful editing, and unflagging support from the beginning; to Lee Levine, Warren Graff, and Mitch Cox, whose considerable comedic talents greatly enhanced many parts of this book; as well as to Lou Kipilman, Danielle Svetcov, Todd Smithline, Max

Zarzana, John Nein, Joshua Swartz, Josh Archibald, Daniel Wasson, and Sarah Schroeder—all of whom provided valuable assistance and shrewd insights during many stages of the writing process.

My family provided not only inspiration but, somewhat inadvertently, much of the field research that helped inform this book. I am grateful for the love and support of my parents, Ken and Caryl, who taught me the value of tolerance and spirited debate, and my brother, Todd, who taught me the importance of defending my position, especially while being hunted with a BB gun. To the DeCastros, a special salute to Mike for embracing his designation as "Uncle Blowhard" with a passion, Lois for her creative inspiration, and Baylee for living the liberal dream. To Jessica and Chris Swanson, Patty, Neil, and the entire Smithline clan, thank you for your loving encouragement and the lively conversations.

I am also endlessly grateful to many friends for their unfailing support: Marty Chester, Dave Uram, Alison Tshangana, David Ziring, Jodi and Andy Brown, Aviva Rosenthal, Liana Schwarz, Alex Kazan, Shannon Farley, Lesley Reidy, Kim Neumann, Lara Abbott, Rebecca Davis, Melody King, Bridgette Bates, Tatyana Tsinberg, Carol Brydolf, the Suffin family, and the numerous other family members and friends who took time to share their political wisdom and partisan horror stories.

I'd also like to acknowledge several important influences who shaped my political and humor sensibilities: Matt Dorf, my former bureau chief, who schooled me in the ways of Washington; Donal Brown, my high school journalism teacher, who showed me how to kill 'em with words; Dave Kreines, a master of both words and wit, and one of the best friends I ever knew; and the late Duane Garrett, one of the funniest commentators and most brilliant political minds of his generation.

And most importantly, I am grateful beyond words to my son, Joel, for helpfully trying to edit drafts of this book in crayon and for laughing at all my jokes; and to my wife, Laura, who inspires me every day. Her abiding faith, brilliant insights, and sharp editing helped make every part of this book better. Together, their love and laughter make every part of life better, too.

About the Author

Daniel Kurtzman chronicles the absurdities of politics as editor of politicalhumor.about.com, the popular website that is part of The New York Times Company's About .com network. As a former Washington correspondent-turned-political satirist, his work has appeared in the *New York Times*, the *Huffington Post*, the *San Francisco Chronicle*, and the *Funny Times*, among other publications. He lives with his wife and their son in the San Francisco Bay Area. An equal opportunity offender, Kurtzman is also the author of *How to Win a Fight with a Liberal*.

www.FightConservatives.com

Facebook: facebook.com/politicalhumor

Twitter: twitter.com/politicalhumor